Laying Foundations

Phase II

Understanding People

Pocket Principles®
and Guided Discussions

For Leaders

Understanding People, Pocket Principles® and Guided Discussions, For Leaders

For copyright information:
Worldwide Discipleship Association
(Attention: Margaret Garner)
P.O. Box 142437
Fayetteville, GA 30214 USA
E-mail: mgarner@disciplebuilding.org
Web Site: www.disciplebuilding.org

Scripture quotations, unless otherwise indicated, are from THE HOLY BIBLE, NEW INTERNATIONAL VERSION®, NIV® Copyright © 1973, 1978, 1984, 2011 by Biblica, Inc.™

Used by permission. All rights reserved worldwide.

NOTE: In an effort to recognize that both men and women are co-heirs of God's grace, we have chosen to use alternating gender pronouns in this document. However, we do recognize and embrace gender-specific roles in Scripture.

Development & Writing Team:
Bob Dukes
Margaret Garner
Jack Larson
Margo Theivagt
Lee Tolar

Publishing Team:
Nila Duffitt
Buddy Eades
Margaret Garner
David Parfitt

Design by Cristina van de Hoeve
doodlingdesigner.com

A Welcome from WDA's President
Worldwide Discipleship Association, Inc.

Hello Friend!

Let me congratulate you on your decision to learn more about Jesus Christ and what it means to follow Him. There is nothing more important or more rewarding than the decision to follow Him and then to grow as a Christian.

These studies will help you get started on your journey with Christ or encourage and instruct you if you are already on this exciting journey. We in WDA want to help you grow and become all you can be in Christ Jesus!

Because you have chosen to lead, we want to do all we can to support you. In addition to the materials provided in this workbook, we would like to also offer you a free download of the Teaching Outlines for *Understanding People*. www.disciplebuilding.org/materials/ understanding-people-teaching-outlines-free-download/

My prayer and confident belief is that "he who began a good work in you will carry it on to completion until the day of Christ Jesus" (Philippians 1:6) so that He is able "to present you before his glorious presence without fault and with great joy." (Jude 1:24) To Him be glory and praise!

May God richly bless you as you strive to grow in Him.

Bob Dukes
President, Worldwide Discipleship Association
Fayetteville, GA 30214

Understanding People
Table of Contents: Leader

What is a Pocket Principle™? Each Pocket Principle™ is a brief essay that focuses on a single topic necessary to the growth and maturity of a believer.

The 10 Pocket Principles®, about *Understanding People*, focus on what it means to be made in God's image, how God is restoring believers and about the role of needs and emotions in the Christian growth process.

Using Pocket Principles® in a Guided Discussion (small group) format:

You will notice that each Pocket Principle™ has a corresponding Guided Discussion. Because the students who are studying *Understanding People* are usually less mature believers, our suggestion is that they **not be required** to read the Pocket Principles® before coming to the Guided Discussion or after the Discussion. At this point in their maturity, it is best that they be given no work to do outside of the group discussion. (For more information about this, go to our website at www.disciplebuilding.org/about/phases-of-christian-growth/2.) Of course, you can mention the purpose of the Pocket Principles® and **invite** students to read them. The content of the Pocket Principles® will reinforce truth learned in the group discussion. Also, if a group member misses a meeting, he can read the corresponding Pocket Principle™ to review the information missed.

Using Bible Readings:

The booklet entitled *Bible Readings for Devotional Use* is for the student to use in her devotional times. (This is the same booklet used in the Cornerstone *Knowing God* and *Growing Spiritually*.) The Bible readings (for a year) focus on the books of *John, Colossians, I John, Genesis, Exodus, Philippians, Jonah* and some of the *Psalms*. These books have been chosen because they emphasize many of the topics studied in the Cornerstone series. If the student has already begun using the *Bible Readings*, she should continue.

Using Pocket Principles® in a Life Coaching (one-one) format:

Pocket Principles® can also be used effectively in an interactive one-one relationship. However, in this arrangement we suggest that the Life Coach (discipler) ask the student to read the Pocket Principle™ beforehand so the material can be discussed during a one-one appointment. All the dynamics mentioned above still apply, and the Life Coach needs to tailor expectations to the maturity of the student. To facilitate interaction, the material contained in the corresponding Guided Discussion-Leaders Edition will help a Life Coach prepare for the appointment. (For more information about preparing for a Life Coaching appointment, please consult the *Life Coaching Manual* at www.disciplebuilding.org/product-category/life-coaching.)

Leader's Instructions
For Using Guided Discussions

The 10 Guided Discussions, about *Understanding People,* focus on what it means to be made in God's image, how God is restoring believers and about the role of needs and emotions in the Christian growth process.

Guided Discussions for small groups play an important role in the growth of a believer with the **major goal being interaction around Scripture.** The goal of disciple building is not just knowledge, but Christlikeness in character and conduct. Therefore, **application is essential.** (Sections "Looking At Real Life" and "Looking at My Life" are application oriented.) At least one-third of the small group discussion time should be spent discussing application of the truth. It is often tempting to get caught up in the content part of the study, but you, as the leader, are responsible to move the group along to application.

A word needs to be said about the relationship between Pocket Principles® and Guided Discussions. The content of both is generally the same, although not identical. These 2 formats provide different ways of presenting the same content, or both can be used to reinforce the content. (Another type of WDA material is Teaching Outlines. These are designed to be used by a teacher who wants to present the content in a lecture format to a larger group. Free Teaching Outlines can be downloaded from www.disciplebuilding.org/materials/understanding-people-teaching-outlines-free-download.

There are two (2) versions of each study: the Leader's version with answers and special notes, and the Student version with questions, but no answers. *Answers and notes to leaders are in gray, italicized text.*

Much of the preparation has been done for you as a leader: topics have been chosen, Scriptures chosen, questions written. However, it is important that you become comfortable with the material so that you will be able to be flexible and focus on the needs of your group. In the *Small Groups Manual* (WDA), you will find information about the practical aspects of group leadership. Please refer to the section titled "Practical Dynamics of Small Group Leadership." This is available from the WDA store at www.disciplebuilding.org/store/leadership-manuals/small-groups-manual.

Created In The Image Of God

Have you ever felt confused and frustrated by the behavior of another person? Or been confused by your own behavior? "Why did I say that?" "Why did I do that?" Understanding people—both ourselves and others—is important to our own personal growth and to our ability to impact the lives of others. This series of Pocket Principles® is designed to help us begin the process of understanding people. We begin with several benefits that understanding people can bring us.

First, understanding people helps us to understand what motivates their behavior. When God created humanity, He created us incomplete, and this incompleteness drives people to try to get their needs met. For example, one of the greatest needs all of us have is for value and worth. We see this need revealed in the ways people seek acceptance, recognition, and approval. From the child's attention-seeking to an adult's basic insecurity, this need is evident. Driven by this need, a child will often act out to get negative attention which is preferable to being ignored. An adult will make all kinds of sacrifices to win some positive feedback and may even demand it from others. Even if we deny our needs, we still are driven by them, and our words and actions betray us.

Second, we need to understand people so we can be sensitive to them. The more we understand people, their struggles and needs, the more we can come along side them in helpful, significant ways, communicate their "specialness" and show them their need for God and spiritual growth.

> Our understanding of people must be derived from the Bible. What does God say about mankind?

A third reason to understand people is to correct inadequate views of humanity. There are many wrong views of mankind both outside of Christianity and within. Our understanding of people must be derived from the Bible. What does God say about mankind? Since God created us, He knows even more about us than we do about ourselves. In the Pocket Principles® that follow we will explore how God has created us, the effect of the Fall of mankind and the restorative ministry of Christ. In this Pocket Principle™ we will begin to define and understand what it means to be made in the image of God.

BIBLICAL TEACHING ABOUT THE IMAGE OF GOD IN MANKIND

Scripture makes many clear statements about the image of God in mankind. The first one is found in Genesis 1:27.

So God created mankind in His own image,
in the image of God He created them,
male and female He created them.

1

Although it seems so, this passage is not redundant. The repetition is a Hebrew expression designed to communicate emphasis and build to a climax. In fact, everything in the creation account builds to a climax: God creates something, steps back from it, admires it and pronounces it "good." He does this over and over until He comes to the creation of humanity.

God saved the best for last. It was as if He said, "Okay, what We have done so far is pretty good, but now We need to do something that is even more spectacular. Let's create humans. We need to make them greater than everything else in all of the universe. Let's do that by creating them in Our image. Let's make them like Us."

Humanity was God's masterpiece, His high point, the climax of creation. Indeed, everything else was made for humans, not God. The rest of creation was to be the place where people would dwell and live and move. People were to rule over, maintain and develop God's creation. Though all other parts of creation bear God's mark and design, only humanity bears His image.

Often Christians don't appreciate the unique place that God has given them.

Psalm 8:3-7 puts it this way:

When I consider Your heavens, the work of Your fingers,
the moon and the stars, which You have set in place,
what is mankind that You are mindful of them,
human beings that You care for them?

You made them a little lower than "elohim"
and crowned them with glory and honor.
You made them rulers over the works of Your hands;
You put everything under their feet:
all flocks and herds, and the beasts of the field,
the birds of the air,
and the fish of the sea, all that swim the paths of the seas.

Christians may become too focused on the problem of sin and lose sight of the dignity of mankind. While it is true that all humans, including those who are believers, have an ongoing serious problem with sin, it is also true that all humanity, including nonbelievers, have been created in God 's image. Psalm 8 tells us that mankind was made just a little lower than "elohim." The Hebrew word "elohim" is the name of God used to reveal His might and sovereignty. It is probably best to understand this passage to be saying that God created humanity just a little lower than Himself. Out of all of creation, humans are the only ones who reflect God's image. There is none other like them.

THE MEANING OF THE IMAGE OF GOD IN MANKIND

Being made in God's image means that we are like God in many ways, but not in all ways. We are like Him in that we have a personality, an intellect, a will and emotions. We are also creative, as He is. Look around and see what humans have done in architecture, art, medicine, science, and technology. We are advancing in our understanding and in our ability to control the world we live in because God has given us the ability to learn, invent and create, to plan and carry out those plans. We communicate with complex, abstract language. No other animal is able to do this, only humans. Humanity alone bears God's image.

God's image is shown in still other ways. Because God is the standard of right and wrong, all people have an inner sense of right and wrong, a moral compass of sorts, a conscience (Romans 2:14-15). People have a spiritual dimension so we are able to have a relationship with God. We have an innate desire to worship God, although at times it may be misdirected toward false gods (Romans 1:21-23). We have deep longings for a better world, deeper relationships and a more meaningful life. We are capable of having significant relationships and joining with others to do incredible feats (like putting a man on the moon) and creating almost unimaginable objects (such as a space station). Humans reflect God more than any other created being.

> Mankind was God's masterpiece, His high point, the climax of creation.

THE RESTORATION OF THE IMAGE OF GOD IN HUMANITY

The Fall of humanity damaged the image of God in people. Although God's image was marred, it was not destroyed (James 3:9). Humanity is like a classic car that has deteriorated, that seems like a piece of junk. It is rusted, dented and broken. It is easy to discount it as something that needs to be discarded. But it is not a piece of junk. It is a classic car desperately in need of restoration. This is how it is with humanity. God's image in them is marred, but they are image-bearers who are desperately in need of restoration.

God sent Christ into the world not just to win our salvation but to restore what has been lost. The goal of the Christian life is to become like Christ. Jesus is the visible image of the invisible God (Colossians 1:15; Hebrews 1:3). So to become like Christ is to restore the image of God in fallen people. This is God's goal, His commitment to us.

Although God is renewing us on the inside (our spiritual selves), the outside (our physical selves) is increasingly wasting away (II Corinthians 4:16). This wasting away of the outside will eventually cause us to die physically. In eternity God will instantly finish the work on the inside, and when Jesus returns to earth, He will also restore the outside. We will have a new body fashioned after Christ's resurrection body that will be suited for the new world that God will create.

> So to become like Christ is to restore the image of God in fallen people. This is God's goal, His commitment to us.

In light of what it means to be created in the image of God, we should celebrate the majesty of mankind. Mankind is God's supreme creation. All people, whether believers or nonbelievers, are created with great worth because they are created in the image of God. It is that image that makes the weak, the downtrodden, the defenseless, the old and the disabled significant. We cannot reject them as the world often does because as image-bearers they reflect Him and represent Him in this world.

While God's image in humanity gives us value, it does not give us salvation. Although all humans were created for eternal life, no one is guaranteed eternal life. It is only as a person comes to a saving faith in Jesus Christ that she receives eternal life and Christ begins to restore God's image in her. As God's image is restored, the person begins to be changed from the inside out. She begins the process of becoming more like Christ and is enabled by God's power and guidance to use her abilities to glorify God and advance His Kingdom. Humanity was created for great things but our true and full purpose cannot be realized without God. The great tragedy of hell is that some who were created in God's image and therefore were destined for great things will spend eternity separated from Him.

There are many significant implications of being created in God's image.

- It should bring forth praise to God for the unique place and abilities that God has given mankind.

- All people have worth and deserve to be treated with dignity and respect.

- It removes all basis for racism or feelings of superiority or inferiority.

- It is the basis for saying that only God has the right to take a life or prescribe when a life should be taken.

- It is the only true basis for having a high view of mankind.

- It provides a basis for the argument that people should play an important role in living the Christian life (Colossians 1:28,29; Philippians 2:12,13), as opposed to God doing it all.

Created In The Image Of God

IMPORTANT to Leader: *Answers and notes to leaders are in gray, italicized text.*

GOAL:

For a disciple to be amazed and appreciative that God has created all people in His image.

GETTING STARTED:

If a person sees himself as "unable to do anything right," how might this affect the way he lives his life?

Fear of failure, hesitancy to try anything new, may do things to sabotage himself, may exaggerate any error he makes, may minimize good he does, etc.

Transition: Having poor self-esteem can have a dramatic effect on a person's life. For this reason, God wants us to see ourselves as people created in His image, which has a positive effect on our lives.

STUDYING TOGETHER:

Read Genesis 1:26-28.

Scripture doesn't explicitly define the "image of God in mankind," but we do know that when the God of the universe entrusted His image to human beings, He gave us incredible worth. Historically, the image of God in mankind has been understood to mean that humans have certain capacities that are like God's.

1. What are some of these capacities?

    Ability to think, ability to appreciate beauty, capable of moral choice, ability to experience intimacy, demonstrate creativity, ability to reason, etc.

2. James 3:9 makes it clear that all people are made in the image of God, believers and non-believers. What are some indications in our society that people, even sinful people, were created in the image of God?

    We see people do good deeds, create beautiful works of art, make brilliant discoveries, etc.

3. According to verse 28 in Genesis 1 what is mankind's relationship to nature, specifically to animals?

They are to rule over every creature of the earth.

4. What do you think are some of the differences between humans and animals?

Humans were created in the image of God and are able to have fellowship with Him. Humans are capable of moral choice and have the capacity to worship God. Humans have authority over animals. Humans are a special creation of God.

5. What is the significance of God making both male and female in His image?

Since there are differences between males and females, it appears that it takes both to fully represent the image of God.

Read Psalm 8:4-8.

6. What place did God give mankind in the creation order?

God gave human beings an exalted place that is a little lower than God.

7. What did God crown mankind with?

Glory and honor.

What do you think that means?

We are the crowning, most important achievement of God's creation. We are to bring glory and honor to Him with our lives.

LOOKING AT REAL LIFE:

Earlier we said, "we do know that when the God of the universe entrusted His image to human beings, He gave us incredible worth."

8. What are some of the implications of this?

God's image in us is permanent, not whimsical; God's love is genuine; God's image is equal in everyone (not just believers), etc.

9. How should this affect a believer's life?

Gives believers confidence and security; tells believers to love and respect non-believers; etc.

10. Discuss some ways you see the likeness of God in others:

    In their conversation:

    In their family life:

    In their interaction with friends and co-workers:

    In their hobbies:

    In their accomplishments:

LOOKING AT MY LIFE:

Psalm 8 exalts God. We can praise and worship Him by praying this Scripture back to Him.

"O Lord, our Lord, how majestic is your name in all the earth!" Psalm 8:9 (NIV)

Leader: Lead the group in praying Psalm 8 to God, focusing on His majesty, glory, creativity, and mankind's relationship to Him.

About Prayer: Since this series of studies is directed toward young believers, we are suggesting that their involvement in group prayer be progressive: from listening to the teacher pray, to participation using simple sentence prayers and on to spontaneous praying. Often young believers have little or no experience with public prayer and may be hesitant to pray aloud. Using a progressive approach will help them become comfortable praying aloud. Be sensitive about where group members are in their development and involve them accordingly. If group members are more mature Christians, of course you may let them participate in the prayer. Tailor the prayer to the maturity and needs of the group.

The Uniqueness Of Each Person

I'm always amazed when I think of how God created a world that's filled with incredible diversity and variety. There are different kinds of colors, tastes, sounds, foods, scenery, animals, ideas, types of leisure… (and the list just goes on and on). But one area that is especially intriguing to me is the variety of people He has created. In fact, everyone is different. There are no two of us alike. We are each special.

In spite of our great diversity, the Bible says that we were all created in the image of God. Therefore, we all have some things in common, things that make up our 'humanness.' We've already noted that all humans have the capacity to think, reason, make decisions, worship, communicate, create, appreciate beauty, etc. We also have similar limitations and needs. We all need food, shelter and clothing. We also need to be loved and to love others. We are also constrained by our physical capacity and strength, knowledge, mortality, and senses, to mention just a few of our limitations.

But do these similarities make us all identical? Not in the least! Though we have certain traits and characteristics that we share, we're also very different from one another. Everyone of us is unique, a one-of-a-kind, special, limited edition! This uniqueness doesn't happen by accident. It's also part of God's grand design and plan. Even our striving to affirm our own identity isn't accidental. When a child pulls away from his parents to assert his own unique personhood, he's really just trying to discover more fully who he really is. This is healthy and normal behavior, part of God's plan for self-awareness.

GOD'S INVOLVEMENT

God forms each one of us lovingly and intentionally. We're not just an "accident-of-nature" (as many atheists and evolutionists would have us believe). There's purpose, planning, and design that led up to our existence. Our parents were certainly involved (obviously), but so was God. Whether our parents rejoiced when they received the news of our pending arrival, or regretted their decision to procreate and conceive, we are here nonetheless, ***because God wanted us here!***

David talks about the unique role that God plays in bringing us into existence in Psalm 139:13-15.

For You created my inmost being;
You knit me together in my mother's womb.
I praise you because I am fearfully and wonderfully made;
Your works are wonderful, I know that full well.

*My frame was not hidden from you
when I was made in the secret place.
When I was woven together in the depths of the earth,
your eyes saw my unformed body.
All the days ordained for me were written in your book
before one of them came to be.*

David has become a voice for each of us, expressing gratitude to God for His creative involvement in making us. God was intentionally involved in making us who we are, both inwardly ("inmost being") and outwardly ("my frame"). The inner man has to do with our personalities, our mind, will, and emotions, our likes and dislikes, our strengths and weaknesses. The outer man is our physical bodies, our appearance, physical strength, natural coordination, etc.

To show God's personal involvement in making us, the Bible uses words and phrases that capture the notion of nurture and creativity: "knit together," "fearfully and wonderfully made," and "woven together." The psalmist also indicates that God created us with a purpose and destiny in mind, even determining the number of days we would live. Though this passage doesn't tell us exactly what that purpose is, elsewhere the Bible makes it clear that we exist to bring glory to God (Ephesians 1:11-12) and to live in a personal and eternal relationship with Him (John 3:16).

Unfortunately, in spite of God's affirmation to the contrary, there are many people who have become convinced that their life is unimportant or useless. Some even consider themselves a burden to society, thinking it would have been better if they had never been born. Nothing could be further from the truth! God has created each of us in a way that is unique and special. Each of us is designed to bring Him glory in a way that no one else can. He wants to accomplish His good works in each of us and through each of us.

Everyone of us is unique, a one-of-a-kind, special, limited edition!!

INDIVIDUAL UNIQUENESS

Some social theorists affirm that children are born as a 'blank slate' and our surroundings alone are responsible for determining who we become. In other words our environment determines who we are. According to Scripture that is not totally true. God makes each person unique in many special ways. While the environment has an ongoing and significant impact on our lives, God wrote on our 'slate' when He created us (Psalm 139:13). He has given us each a unique personality as well as natural strengths and weaknesses. He has given us unique abilities as well, such as hand-eye coordination, ability to play an instrument, artistic ability, intelligence, etc.

When we become a Christian, God's creative work in our lives begins again in a different way. When we trust Christ, God gives each of us spiritual gifts through the person of His Holy Spirit. These abilities enable us to have a unique ministry to believers and unbelievers (I Corinthians 12:7). In fact, most of us have a combination of several gifts. These gifts become evident as we go about helping others in effective and enjoyable service. God also calls us to specific ministries where we are able to employ our special gifts in ways distinct from others. For example, Paul was called to have a ministry to the Gentiles while Peter was called to have a ministry to the Jews (Galatians 2:8). Sometimes He will even change our ministries as we mature.

> [God] wants to accomplish His good works in each of us and through each of us.

God continues to bring about change in us throughout life. He employs agents that work internally (the Holy Spirit and the Scriptures) and agents that work externally (angels, circumstances) to conform us to the image of Christ. There are other forces that God uses to shape us, but one of the most profound is the influence of our family. This environment creates a climate for both good and bad in our lives. It takes wisdom and maturity to process this influence in a healthy way. Fortunately, God assures us that He can even use the bad to bring good into our lives (Romans 8:28). He uses all of our experiences, even the unique culture and era that we live in, to bring us to Christ and to mature us (Acts 17:26-28).

CONCLUSION

God has made each of us special and unique. He's created us in amazing ways and made it possible for us to contribute to what He's doing in this world. Every person who comes to Christ brings something that no one else is able to offer. Rather than making us arrogant, this knowledge should cause us to remain humble as we celebrate our special place and affirm God's sovereign plan for us.

The Uniqueness Of Each Person

2

IMPORTANT to Leader: Answers and notes to leaders are in gray, italicized text.

GOAL:

For a disciple to appreciate her own positive uniqueness as a person created in the image of God.

GETTING STARTED:

Imagine that the world has no colors. Everything is black or white or shades of gray. What do you think the effect would be on us?

Would decrease our ability to distinguish between items/people; we couldn't appreciate depth and contrast in the same way, it would be boring and depressing, language would be more limited (no color words), would have less variation, etc.

Transition: Fortunately, God is creative and didn't make things just black and white. One of the ways He has shown His love for diversity is by creating each person a unique being.

STUDYING TOGETHER:

Read Psalm 139:13-16.

1. What do these verses say about God's involvement in making us each who we are?

   He is the Author of our lives; the Planner of our existence.

2. What do you think David meant by "inmost being" (vs. 13)?

   The term that David uses means "kidneys." This is a Hebrew idiom that refers to the center of our emotions and also to our moral sensitivity. Not only did God design my outward appearance, but He was also shaping my personality.

3. Why did David praise God in verse 14?

   He praised God for the way he was formed in His mother's womb. David gave praise because he knew God didn't see him as an afterthought, but rather a wonderful creation.

4. David considered God's creative "works" as "wonderful." As you think about your personality and the way your body functions, would you consider God's creative work in you as "wonderful"? Why or why not?

5. Even though all people are made in God's image, we are all unique. Which of the following categories of differences apply to all people and which ones apply only to Christians?

Spiritual gifts and spiritual calling apply to Christians. The others apply to everyone.

☐ roles

☐ personality

☐ spiritual gifts

☐ passion

☐ talent

☐ spiritual calling

☐ physical appearance

Leader: At this Phase (Phase II) we mention spiritual gifts, but do not emphasize them or talk with disciples about finding their spiritual gifts. Believers need to get grounded in their relationship with Jesus before thinking about their gifts used to serve the Body. If a question arises, it should be answered but an in depth discussion should be deferred until later.

Read Revelation 5:9-10.

6. According to these verses, is this uniqueness true of every person on the earth?

Yes. We are all unique in that we originate from different families, experience different cultures, speak different languages, live in different communities, and are citizens of different nations.

Read Colossians 2:10.

7. According to this verse, what does Christ bring?

Christ brings our lives "fullness, completeness." Although we have all been uniquely created in God's image, we are incomplete without Christ.

LOOKING AT REAL LIFE:

8. What would the world be like if we were all the same? What is the value of diversity?

LOOKING AT MY LIFE:

Leader: Provide sheets of paper with a different group member's name at the top of each one. Have the group pass around the pages one at a time. As each page is passed, each person is to write down one positive thing they observe about that person that is unique.

When everyone has written down one positive thing about each person, read each person's sheet aloud to the group. Give the person the sheet of paper when you are finished.

When explaining the exercise, make sure you emphasize "uniqueness" as the focus of their positive comments. This should be a tremendously affirming time for your group. Have fun!

Close the time in prayer with anyone who feels comfortable praying aloud doing so using sentence prayers. (One sentence stating a praise to God, or a request, or a thanksgiving, etc.)

The Impact Of The Fall

If mankind is created in the image of God, why do we struggle with so many problems? Why do people have so much trouble getting along? Why are there so many wars? Why are people so selfish? These and many questions like them betray the fact that there is something wrong with humanity. Though we started out well, something happened along the way that upset the apple cart, and we have never fully recovered.

In the first book of the Bible, Genesis, there is a record of Adam and Eve in the Garden of Eden, and we learn what happened to human beings that has caused so many problems. We can only imagine that the garden was a beautiful, lush place filled with all kinds of vegetation and animals. The weather was perfect, and there was plenty to eat. There were also opportunities to explore and learn. Everyone got along well, and God was at their "beck and call."

God had given them only one restriction. They could eat from any tree in the garden except from the tree in the middle of the garden: the tree of the knowledge of good and evil (Genesis 2:8-9,15-17). God told Adam that if he were to eat from that tree he would die.

In Genesis 3 another character enters the garden—Satan in the form of a talking serpent. His purpose was to try to persuade Adam and Eve to eat the fruit from the forbidden tree. In a very clever way the serpent called God's character into question and caused Eve to doubt God's goodness (Genesis 3:1-6). He convinced Eve to try the fruit, and she, in turn, convinced Adam to join her, and nothing has been the same since.

What happened as a result of Adam and Eve's sin is often called the Fall of mankind. We became less than we were created to be. Before the Fall, human beings desired to know and follow God. Afterward, attitudes were hostile toward God (Romans 8:5-8). This inclination against God is what the Bible calls a sin nature (Galatians 5:19-21). Mankind's hostility or indifference toward God leads to many sinful behaviors. As a result of the Fall, we human beings are thoroughly sinful and unable to make our way back to God. We are lost and unable to save ourselves. This does not mean that human beings are as bad as we can possibly be.

All of mankind was impacted by Adam and Eve's sin. The following are three ways human life was affected by Adam and Eve's choices.

PHYSICAL DEATH

God told Adam and Eve that if they ate the fruit from the tree of the knowledge of good and evil they would surely die. They did eat, and although they did not die immediately, they did begin to die. Their physical death had become certain. The only question was how long they would live before they died. And they were not the only ones who would die. Death spread to all people because all sinned (Romans 5:12). So through the sin of one man, sin spread to all people, and all people died.

SEPARATION FROM GOD

Separation from God is spiritual death. Mankind's relationship with God died with the Fall, and we were separated from God, the source of all life. Thus, human beings would not only die physically but also spiritually, leaving us to wander around aimlessly looking for something that was missing—looking for life from God.

Many people realize there is something missing in life and are searching for something more or better. But they don't know what it is. It is God. Even when we do have a relationship with God and life is better, there is still a sense that something is missing. We will never fully experience life and fulfillment until we go to be with Jesus and experience life beyond our imagination. We look forward to that day with a deep yearning. But it begins with finding life now through a relationship with the living God.

> Although fallen, humans are still capable of doing good because we are created in the image of God.

Physical life moves from life to death, but spiritual life moves from death to life (John 5:24). We were all born dead spiritually and only find life through Jesus Christ. That is why Jesus told Nicodemus he had to be born again (John 3:3). All human beings are born dead spiritually, and their need is to come to life by becoming alive to God.

CHANGED RELATIONSHIPS

The Fall changed people's relationships in many ways. It changed their relationship with themselves, other people and even with nature. We are told that before the Fall, the man and the woman were naked but not ashamed (Genesis 2:25). But immediately after the Fall, they realized they were naked and were ashamed (Genesis 3:7). Shame altered their relationship with themselves. This is true of all of us. All of us now struggle, to some degree, with self-worth because of our sin. One of our greatest needs is to regain a sense of our value and worth.

Even mankind's relationship with nature was affected by the Fall. The world itself was altered. Originally the earth produced all kinds of fruit. After the Fall, fruit production was more difficult. God cursed the ground and caused thorns and thistles to grow to crowd out the crops people needed to live. Human beings would have to work hard to survive in this new world (Genesis 3:17-19). All of creation, we are told in Scripture, was subjected to frustration through the Fall and awaits its liberation from decay that will occur when God's children are liberated (Romans 8:19-21).

The Fall of mankind was like a tragic train wreck. It left humanity and this world battered and in twisted disarray. A train wreck can be cleaned up and cleared away. The condition of humanity and of this world will not be fixed completely until Christ returns to make everything right. When a person comes into a personal relationship with Christ, Christ begins the process of restoration that will continue throughout the person's whole life. But the restoration will not be completed in this lifetime, and so we look forward to Christ's return and the completion of the good work He has begun in us.

The Fall of mankind and its terrible consequences are not a pretty story. But it does help us make some sense out of this world and explains why there is so much pain and suffering. It also helps us to develop realistic expectations in an imperfect world

The Impact Of The Fall

3

IMPORTANT to Leader: *Answers and notes to leaders are in gray, italicized text.*

GOAL:

For a disciple to begin to understand why he struggles with sin.

GETTING STARTED:

Which of the following mischievous acts did you do as a child? Share with the group.

☐ Sneaked into a movie or ball game

☐ Shoplifted something from a store

☐ Fought with a sibling and then lied to stay out of trouble

☐ Broke something in your house and then tried to hide it

☐ Sneaked out of your house at night while others were sleeping

☐ Used tobacco without your parent's knowledge

☐ other: _____

Transition: *As a child, our natural inclination was to often act against God's principles. This is just one of the effects of the Fall. In today's lesson, we will look at the impact of the fall in our lives and begin to gain an understanding of why we struggle with sin.*

STUDYING TOGETHER:

Note: Because there are so many Scripture verses in this lesson, assign different group members each of the passages to read before the lesson begins. This will decrease the amount of time spent looking for passages. (To read: Genesis 3:8; Romans 8:5-8; Romans 5:8,10,12; Galatians 5:19-21; Ephesians 2:1,12.)

Read Genesis 3:8.

1. After Adam and Eve chose to disobey God and fall into sin, according to Genesis 3:8, were they drawn to God or did they run from God?

   They not only ran from God, they tried to hide from Him as well. In fact, God came looking for them.

Read Romans 8:5-8 & Romans 5:8,10.

2. What do these verses say about mankind's nature after the Fall?

   Before the Fall, mankind's nature was inclined toward God or at least neutral towards Him. Now it is hostile toward God.

Read Galatians 5:19-21.

3. What does this passage indicate about mankind's basic inclination after the Fall?

   Mankind's basic inclination away from God (sin nature) leads to sinful behaviors.

Read Ephesians 2:12.

4. What does this verse say about humanity's condition after the Fall?

   The Fall put human beings in a condition in which they were thoroughly sinful, lost and unable to make their way back to God.

Read Genesis 3:1-7; Romans 5:12; Ephesians 2:1.

5. According to these verses in Genesis and Romans, how did the Fall affect human beings physically?

   When Adam and Eve disobeyed God, they began to die physically. Adam's sin and resulting death spread to all people because all have sinned.

6. According to the Ephesians verse, how did the Fall affect people spiritually?

   Separation from God is spiritual death. Because humans are spiritually dead they have no capacity to relate to God.

Read Genesis 3:7-19.

7. According to Genesis 3:7-10, how did the Fall change mankind's relationship with himself?

   Because of the Fall, shame enters into mankind's relationship with himself. All of us (as sinners) struggle with self worth because of our shame about our sin. One of the greatest needs all human beings have is to regain a sense of their own value and worth.

8. According to Genesis 3:11-13, how did the Fall affect the way we relate to others?

   Sin severely damages the way human beings relate to others. Note the change in the way Adam and Eve related to one another in these verses.

9. According to Genesis 3:17-19, how did the Fall affect nature?

   Nature also became corrupted because of the Fall of mankind. Note the curses in this passage.

LOOKING AT REAL LIFE:

10. Give specific examples of how the Fall has impacted the following:

- our physical bodies: *diseases, birth defects, aging, death, etc.*

- our relationship with God: *has separated us from Him, makes us fearful of Him, causes us to hide from Him because of shame, etc.*

- our relationship with ourselves: *insecurity, shame, suicide, etc.*

- our relationships with others: *poor communication, anger, lack of intimacy, etc.*

LOOKING AT MY LIFE:

What is the one area of your life in which you are experiencing struggle with your sinful nature? As you think about that area, write out a prayer to God asking Him to give you strength to overcome this struggle in your life.

Leader: When group members finish their written prayers, lead them in praying sentence prayers thanking God for His goodness, mercy, patience, love and initiative in spite of our rebellion.

Reversing The Effects Of The Fall

The Fall of mankind was like having an atomic bomb go off near Eden. Adam and Eve survived, but because they were exposed to the radiation, they were greatly deformed and sickened. It was as if they were altered genetically, and all their offspring for all generations would be affected.

All human beings have been affected by the Fall. They no longer love God and the things of God but have become hostile toward Him. The Bible indicates that as a result of the Fall, all people have received a sin nature. Paul in Romans 8 describes how this fallen nature affects everyone. "Those who live according to the flesh have their minds set on what the flesh desires…The mind governed by the flesh is death…the mind governed by the flesh is hostile to God, it does not submit to God's law, nor can it do so." (Romans 8:5-7)

> God brings about a radical inward change when a person repents of her sin and submits to Him.

A reasonable question in light of this is, "Has the image of God in humans been destroyed?" The answer is no. God's image was defaced and damaged, but it was not obliterated. The Bible continues to speak of humans as being in God's image and admonishes all people to treat others with dignity and respect because everyone still reflects God's image to some degree (James 3:9; I Corinthians 11:7).

Because of the Fall, all people are lost and unable to respond to God. There is a desperate need to reverse the effects of the Fall. And God, in His graciousness and love, has set in motion all that is needed to gradually reverse these effects through two initiatives.

REFORMATION

The first initiative we call reformation. Humanity is in need of a radical change of heart: hostility toward God needs to be changed to love; a sense of alienation from God needs to be changed to a sense of acceptance by Him; a natural inclination away from God needs to be changed to a desire toward Him. But people cannot change themselves. They cannot reverse the effects of the Fall. There is nothing in this world that can change them. This world says that people can be changed through education or political views or their own will. Though there is some truth in these views, none of these can change or heal a heart that has turned against God.

Only God can change a person's heart. God brings about a radical inward change when a person repents of sin and submits to Him. Ezekiel the prophet describes this radical inward change in this way:

I will sprinkle clean water on you and you will be clean; I will cleanse you from all your impurities and from all your idols. I will give you a new heart and put a new spirit in you; I will remove from you your heart of stone and give you a heart of flesh. And I will put my Spirit in you and move you to follow my decrees and be careful to keep my laws. (Ezekiel 36:25-27)

Christians usually notice evidence of this change of heart shortly after their conversion. They find new desires within themselves. They want to pray and seek God while in the past they did not have time for God. They seek to be around other believers and have a new desire to understand God's Word and to follow Him. They often have a new inward sense that they are children of God. One of the most surprising things that happened to me when I came to Christ was that I was changed from a totally self-centered person to a person who really cared about other people. I have no explanation for this change except that God invaded my life and changed me. God changed my heart.

> God has set out to transform us. Apart from His work in our lives we would never be able to change.

RESTORATION

The second initiative of God toward us we call restoration. Even though He changed our hearts at salvation, He now needs to change our lives by restoring the defaced image of God in us. Paul refers to this in Colossians 3:10 when he says you, "have put on the new self, which is being renewed in knowledge in the image of its Creator." This is the process of renewing that begins when we come to know Christ personally, and continues throughout our lives.

We are being restored to Christlikeness. Jesus is the visible expression (image) of the invisible God, so to be made into Christ's image is to be made into the image of God. This process begins at salvation and goes on throughout our lifetime. Then when we die and go to be with Jesus, God instantly finishes the project. Thus, the effects of the Fall will not be totally reversed in our lifetime, but God will bring to completion that which He has begun in us (Philippians 1:6).

The restoration process has two parts. The first is growth in our relationship with Christ which is accomplished as we spend time with God and His people seeking Him, learning about Him and His ways and applying His Word to our lives. The second part of restoration is healing from the damage of sin. We all come into the Christian life damaged by living in a fallen world and by the sinful choices we have made. We have all been hurt in our lives and often have little insight about how to heal from those hurts. Often, the need people have to heal from emotional damage has not been well recognized in the church, but it is clearly part of Christ's message of hope to us.

At the very beginning of His ministry, Jesus quotes from Isaiah 61:1-3 (Luke 4:18-19) which refers to the healing aspect of His ministry.

The Spirit of the Sovereign Lord is on me, because the Lord has anointed me to preach good news to the poor. He has sent me to bind up the brokenhearted, to proclaim freedom for the captives and release from darkness for the prisoners, to proclaim the year of the Lord's favor and the day of vengeance of our God, to comfort all who mourn, and provide for those who grieve in Zion—to bestow on them a crown of beauty instead of ashes, the oil of gladness instead of mourning, and a garment of praise instead of a spirit of despair. They will be called oaks of righteousness, a planting of the Lord for the display of His splendor. (Isaiah 61:1-3)

Jesus came to set us free from the damage that sin has done in our lives. The damage from our past sinful choices and sinful treatment by others may take many forms: addictions, depression, a distorted self-image, relational problems, unhealthy thinking patterns, unresolved emotional problems or many other difficulties. These problems have roots in unresolved pain from our past, and to get better a person must process that pain and replace unhealthy behaviors with healthy ones. This takes time and help from others who understand the healing process. Notice that healing is a process and does not occur instantly at salvation.

God has set out to transform us. Apart from His work in our lives we would never be able to change. He has to reform us by changing our hearts and then restore us by giving us the strength and direction to become more like Christ. Apart from God's work in a person's life there is no hope of a better, more meaningful life.

Reversing The Effects Of The Fall

4

IMPORTANT to Leader: *Answers and notes to leaders are in gray, italicized text.*

GOAL:

For a disciple to be fully convinced of her need for God's intervention to reverse the effects of the Fall in her life.

GETTING STARTED:

Imagine that you are enjoying your beautiful new home. Then, bad news! You find termites, and extensive termite damage in one wall of the living room. What kind of steps do you need to take to restore your home to its original condition?

To Leader: Among other answers, these 3 important points need to be made: Get rid of the termites, keep new termites from getting in and repair the damage.

Transition: *As termites damaged your house, sin damages us, and there is a need to take steps to repair the damage in our lives.*

STUDYING TOGETHER:

The Fall of mankind caused great damage and its repercussions are still being felt today. However, it is important to understand that although the image of God in human beings was greatly defaced, it was not completely obliterated (James 3:9).

1. According to **Colossians 1:21**, what effect does the Fall have on the way mankind views God?

    Mankind has an internal bias (hostility, alienation) against God.

Read Romans 3:9-18.

2. Is there anything in these verses that indicates that, on their own, people can change themselves and reverse the effects of the Fall? Why or why not?

    No. Humans do not have the power or resources to overcome the effects of the Fall on their own, nor do they have the will or motivation. Many people think change can be brought about through education, political activism, religiosity, etc.

3. Name some infomercials designed to reverse the physical, psychological, spiritual, or relational effects of the Fall.

    Some examples might include: miracle skin creams, exercise equipment, psychics, nutritional supplements, etc.

Although some of these gadgets and methods may have some merit, they are unable to change people on the inside.

Read Ezekiel 36:26.

4. According to this verse, what is God able to do?

    God can change the human heart.

5. What happens when God changes a heart?

    The person is forgiven, inclined toward God; is friendly to God, wants to love and follow God (Colossians 1:2).

Read Acts 3:19 and II Peter 1:3,5ff.

6. According to Acts 3:19, when does God bring about this radical change?

    When a person repents of his sin and submits to God.

7. According to II Peter 1:3,5ff. what else is needed to further reverse the damages of sin?

    We need to continue growing as believers. Reversing the damages of sin is a process.

8. There are two dimensions to our restoration:

    a. Growth in a relationship with Christ

    According to **Colossians 1:15**, who is equated with the "image of God"?

    Jesus

    According to **II Corinthians 3:18**, what should the process of restoration develop in our lives?

    Christlikeness.

What does this mean?

This means that we become like Christ in His human conduct and character, not in His divine conduct and character.

b.   Healing from the damages of our sin and the sin of others

Compare **Isaiah 61:1-4** with **Luke 4:17-21**. What was an important part of Christ's ministry?

To heal the damages of sin by fixing broken hearts, delivering people from bondage, helping people gain new perspective, comforting those who are sad, etc.

LOOKING AT REAL LIFE:

9.   What are some examples of the damage of sin that needs to be healed in people's lives?

Addictions, depression, distorted self-image, relational problems, unhealthy thinking patterns, unresolved emotional problems, etc.

LOOKING AT MY LIFE:

Write a few sentences describing the areas in your life that need growth or healing that will lead to restoration. Remember, by restoration, we mean the process where we are being renewed into Christlikeness, specifically His character and conduct.

Areas of your character:

Areas of your conduct:

Discuss how you have seen God begin this process of restoration in these areas.

Leader: Praise God for His willingness to restore our lives and make us more like Him. Then encourage group members to pray silently and ask Him to bring restoration to a specific area of their lives they have identified.

Experiencing The Benefits Of Knowing Christ

We often hear about people whose lives hang in the balance because of their damaged hearts. They need a new heart to continue living and cling to life while waiting for a heart donor. All of mankind has a similar condition. Everyone needs a new spiritual heart because the one we have is not open to God or interested in Him.

By God's grace He offers us a new heart. He sent His very own son, Jesus Christ, as a willing donor. Jesus wants to replace our heart of stone with a heart of flesh, a heart that is responsive to God (Ezekiel 36:25-27). Actually, He wants to do much more than this. He wants to give us salvation, make us a part of His family, bring about our healing, enable our spiritual growth and bring us to heaven.

> Jesus wants to replace our heart of stone with a heart of flesh, a heart that is responsive to God.

All of these blessings are possible because Jesus Christ came to this earth and died for our sins on the cross. We deserved to die, but He died in our place. Peter said it very clearly, "For Christ died for sins once for all, the righteous for the unrighteous, to bring you to God." (I Peter 3:18) Christ's death and resurrection from the dead created the possibility of the redemption of all mankind. Now it is up to us to respond and receive the gracious gift God offers. For those who repent by turning from their sins, turning to Christ and trusting Him for salvation, all that God offers will be theirs. Once a person has received God's grace and enters into salvation, God begins the process of transforming that person into the likeness of Christ. In doing this, God is restoring His fallen image in mankind. He is reversing the effects of the Fall.

MANKIND IS NOW MADE ALIVE SPIRITUALLY.

Human beings, who were dead spiritually, are made alive through personal salvation. Paul describes what God has done in his letter to the Ephesians.

As for you, you were dead in your transgressions and sins, in which you used to live when you followed the ways of this world and of the ruler of the kingdom of the air, the spirit who is now at work in those who are disobedient. All of us also lived among them at one time, gratifying the cravings of our sinful nature and following its desires and thoughts. Like the rest, we were by nature objects of wrath. But because of His great love for us, God, who is rich in mercy, made us alive with Christ even when we were dead in transgressions—it is by grace you have been saved.
(Ephesians 2:1-4)

To be alive spiritually means that we are able to relate to God and experience a special relationship with Him as our loving Father. This new relationship with God saves us from His wrath and will last for eternity. God will never tire of us. And we will never tire of Him. This relationship, like any other, grows as we invest time in it. We have not only gained an eternal loving Father, but we have also become part of a whole new family, the family of God. He is the Father, and we who believe are His children (John 1:12).

HUMAN BEINGS CAN NOW CHOOSE TO DO WHAT IS RIGHT.

Human beings, who were enslaved to sin before being made alive spiritually, can now choose to do what is right. We did not lose the ability to choose at the Fall. Rather, we came under the negative influences of our own sin nature, the world and the continuing deceptions of Satan. These influences confuse our minds so that we regularly choose wrong and are blinded to our sinful human condition.

Christ has changed all that. We have been enlightened and delivered from enslavement to sin (Romans 6:6). Through our new relationship with Christ, we can now find wisdom and strength to choose to do what is right. God has given us the Spirit of truth, the Holy Spirit, to live in us and to empower us to live for Him. The Holy Spirit together with the Bible and the people of God show us truth so we can make good choices in our lives, choices that are right and bring glory to God.

This is not to say that we will always make the right choices or do the right things. We can still choose to do what is wrong. In fact, all our old enemies (our sin nature, the world and Satan) are still trying to deceive us and blind us. We are in a spiritual battle in this world, and our enemies are formidable. But Christ is greater and stronger than they are. As we learn to depend on Him and mature spiritually, we will increasingly overcome these enemies; but this battle is an ongoing one, one that will continue throughout this life.

HUMAN BEINGS NOW HAVE CONFIDENCE BEFORE GOD.

Human beings, who were shamed when they were spiritually dead, can now have confidence before God. Since the Fall, we have had a problem with sin and the resulting guilt. We are not able to live up to our own standards, and deep in our hearts, we know it. There are many ways we try to cover our guilt, but they are generally unsuccessful.

Jesus came to take that guilt away. His death was sufficient to satisfy God's wrath against all sins: past, present and future. He removed the barrier of sin that was between God and us, and now, nothing separates the believer from God.

Paul put it this way, "Therefore, there is now no condemnation for those who are in Christ Jesus." (Romans 8:1)

The concept that we are fully and totally forgiven, even when we continue to sin, is a difficult concept to accept. Satan and our consciences continually condemn us and tell us that God certainly cannot love sinners like us. We need to focus on the truth: there is no sin too great to be forgiven, and Jesus has come to cleanse our guilty consciences. Therefore we can approach God's throne of grace with confidence. In fact, God tells us to do that very thing. He instructs us to approach Him with confidence in our times of need (Hebrews 4:16) and to pursue Him aggressively.

Ask and it will be given to you; seek and you will find; knock and the door will be opened to you. For everyone who asks receives; the one who seeks finds; and the one who knocks, the door will be opened. Which of you, if your son asks for bread, will give him a stone? Or if he asks for a fish, will give him a snake? If you then, though you are evil, know how to give good gifts to your children, how much more will your Father in heaven give good gifts to those who ask Him!
(Matthew 7:7-11)

A PERSON IS NOW MADE ONE WITH OTHER BELIEVERS.

People who were at odds with their fellow humans, are now made one with other believers. Needless to say, humanity's treatment of others has generally been less than admirable. As cultures move farther and farther away from Christ they become increasingly ruthless (Romans 1:18-32). There have only been 144 years of recorded history when there hasn't been some kind of a war going on.

There is no sin too great to be forgiven, and Jesus has come to cleanse our guilty consciences.

Jesus came to reconcile us not only to God but also to one another. He has leveled the playing field and removed reasons for prejudice by dying for all people. Everyone comes to Him on the same terms; He makes no distinction between races, sexes or any other classes of people. All who come to Him join the same family of God and have equal access to the Father. Christians are a multinational group of people who find their commonality in Christ. The oneness they share implies intimacy, agreement, companionship and teamwork. Christians have shown over and over that they can demonstrate these qualities with other believers no matter what other differences may be present.

Revelation speaks of our common heritage and inheritance in Christ.

You are worthy to take the scroll and open its seals, because You were slain, and with Your blood You purchased for God persons from every tribe and language and people and nation. You have made them to be a kingdom and priests to serve our God, and they will reign on the earth.
(Revelation 5:9-10)

SUMMARY

God, through Christ, reverses many of the effects of the Fall. He takes away our spiritual deadness, our slavery to sin, our shame and our hostility toward one another. He replaces them with spiritual aliveness, the ability to choose right, confidence before God and oneness with one another. The reversal of these effects begins at salvation and continues as we grow spiritually. Finally, when Christ returns for His people and sets up His Kingdom, all the effects of the Fall will be removed and replaced with something far better than we can imagine. We have a great hope and a great future!

Experiencing The Benefits Of Knowing Christ

GOAL:

For a disciple to fully experience the benefits that result in his life from Christ's death and resurrection.

GETTING STARTED:

Your employer wants to reward you for the great job you've been doing. Being in a generous mood, your employer has given you a choice of one of the following increases in benefits. Which one would you choose?

☐ Salary increase of 25%

☐ Quadruple your current amount of annual paid vacation time

☐ Free use of the corporate jet every weekend and during vacation

Transition: In today's lesson, we will study how Christ's death and resurrection benefits us.

STUDYING TOGETHER:

Note to leader: In the following study, assign the verses below to different group members so you can get everyone involved in the study and save time. It is not necessary for everyone to look up every verse. Verses to assign: Ephesians 2:1-5; Romans 8:9-11; Romans 8:15-16; Romans 6:23; Romans 7:21-23; Romans 6:6; Galatians 5:16,17; Hebrews 4:16, 9:14, 10:22; Ephesians 2:14-18; Galatians 3:28; Ephesians 4:4-6,32.

Let's study four ways we benefit from Christ's death and resurrection.

Benefit #1: Through the death and resurrection of Christ, we can *relate to God.*

Because of the Fall, mankind was dead spiritually. What do the following verses indicate about us being made alive spiritually?

Ephesians 2:1-5

Through personal salvation we have been made alive to God.

Romans 8:9-11

God gives us life through the indwelling Spirit.

Romans 8:15-16

We are able to experience a special relationship with God as our loving Father and are included in His family.

Romans 6:23

This new relationship with God has saved us from His wrath and will last for eternity.

Benefit #2: Through the death and resurrection of Christ, we can *choose to do what is right*.

Because of the Fall, mankind was enslaved to sin. What do the following verses indicate about us being freed from sin to make right choices?

Romans 6:23a

Salvation delivered us from the penalty of sin—death.

Romans 7:21-23

Salvation has not delivered us from the presence of sin, and therefore, we still sin because we have a sin nature.

Romans 6:6; Galatians 5:16

As believers we are no longer slaves to sin and therefore, can say "no" to sin and "yes" to God.

Galatians 5:17

Because sinful desires remain in the believer, a battle with sin continues as long as we remain in these mortal bodies. Though the believer can "sin less" as she grows spiritually, she will never become "sinless" in this life.

Benefit #3: Through the death and resurrection of Christ, *we can boldly approach God because we're not ashamed.*

Because of the Fall, mankind was shamed. What do the following verses indicate about the confidence we should now have before God?

> **Hebrews 9:14, 10:22**
>
> *Christ has cleansed our guilty consciences.*
>
> **Hebrews 4:16, 10:22**
>
> *We can approach God with confidence because the guilt of sin has been removed.*

Benefit #4: Through the death and resurrection of Christ, *we can enjoy unity with other believers.*

Because of the Fall, mankind was at odds with his fellow man. What do the following verses indicate about how we are made "one" with other believers?

> **Ephesians 2:14-18; Galatians 3:28**
>
> *He removes barriers between believers of different groups.*
>
> **Ephesians 4:4-6**
>
> *He allows believers to share in the same spiritual blessings.*
>
> **Ephesians 4:32**
>
> *He enables believers to forgive others because He has forgiven them.*

LOOKING AT REAL LIFE:

What difference will it make in a believer's life if she does not take advantage of these benefits?

Her Christian life will be anemic and frustrating. She will feel isolated, spiritually dull, hopeless, powerless.

LOOKING AT MY LIFE:

Which one of the benefits associated with Jesus' death and resurrection are you experiencing the least in your life right now?

☐ Relating to God

☐ Choosing to do what is right

☐ Approaching God boldly because you're not ashamed

☐ Enjoying unity with other believers

Write out a personal prayer to God, asking Him to help you realize that particular benefit in your life. If there is time, share with the group the benefit you wrote about.

6 Created With Needs

All of God's creation is interdependent in some way: the food chain demonstrates interdependence for nourishment; the life cycles of plants and animals demonstrates interdependence for reproduction, and so on. Humanity, as a part of God's creation, is interdependent with the rest of creation. We are dependent on air to survive, dependent on plants and animals for food, dependent on other people for companionship. God created us this way. In essence, He created us incomplete so that we would have needs!

One of the reasons God created us this way is to show us our need for Him and to move us toward Him as the One who can provide for all our needs. Every one of us can probably point to specific felt needs in our lives that brought us to the point of pursuing God. And without any sense of our needs we would not have pursued Him.

> Every one of us can probably point to specific felt needs in our lives that brought us to the point of pursuing God.

Problems arise when people try to get their needs met apart from God's design, either through inappropriate relationships, substance abuse, materialism, or an endless list of activities which do not satisfy or nourish us but do, rather, hurt us. In order to avoid these destructive behaviors, Christians sometimes resort to denying or minimizing the fact that they have any needs. It is important that we accept the fact that we have needs and that we learn how to meet them appropriately.

Even if we deny our needs, they motivate us anyway. Through many of our activities (both good and bad) we are actually trying to get our needs met. For instance, women read romance novels and men look at pornography to create a fantasy world in their minds, rather than having the real relationships they crave. In fact, by focusing on these fantasies, they may develop expectations and ideas about relationships that are unrealistic and harmful. At the same time, they miss out on the better ways that God uses to meet their needs.

There are many kinds of needs: physical, spiritual, psychological, social, etc. with our physical needs being the most obvious. Without oxygen we would literally die within a few minutes. We can only survive a few days without water and a few weeks without food. Our spiritual, psychological, and social needs may not be as obvious but are also critically important to our overall well-being. We can get a better understanding of our primary needs by looking at the way God created us and how He has provided for these needs.

CREATED WITH A NEED FOR A PERSONAL RELATIONSHIP WITH GOD

One of our greatest needs is for a personal relationship with God. After God created Adam and Eve, He related to them on a personal basis (Genesis 2:19, 3:8-9). Both of them were aware of God's presence and conversed with Him. After the Fall, people continued to seek a relationship with their Creator. This is seen in all cultures by people's propensity to place gods in their lives in an attempt to reach the true God they long to know (Romans 1:21-23). This is also demonstrated by the fact that God has continued to pursue a relationship with people after the Fall and has provided a way for each of us to come back into fellowship with Him (John 6:44; I Peter 3:18).

There are certain needs that only God can meet. He is the only one who could provide a way of salvation for us (I Peter 3:18). He is the only one who could remove the barriers that prevented us from having a relationship with Him (Colossians 2:13-14). He is the only one who could draw us to Himself (John 6:44). Blaise Pascal, the famous French scientist and philosopher, said, "There is a God-shaped vacuum in the heart of each man that can only be filled by Jesus Christ."

> It is important that we accept the fact that we have needs and that we learn how to meet them appropriately.

CREATED WITH A NEED FOR VALUE AND WORTH

Another need we all share is the need to know that we have value and worth. Both theologians and psychologists agree that all people feel a deep desire to be valued by God, other people, and themselves. Because people were created in God's image (Genesis 1:26-28), we do have worth and value (Psalm 8:4-5). Even after the Fall, all people (including non-Christians) continue to bear God's image, even though it is marred (James 3:9). Therefore, people have value and worth whether they realize it or not.

Unfortunately, many believers don't realize that they have inherent value and worth and therefore, seek to be assured of their value and worth from people who can't give assurance or give it inconsistently. Often they seek it from parents who may be overly critical or distant and who are unable to give them what they need. Understanding that God has created us in His image and that He paid the price to reconcile us to Himself is the only consistent way to realize what tremendous value we have.

CREATED WITH A NEED FOR IMPACT

An important need that is also identified by both religious leaders and psychologists is our deep desire for purpose in this life. All of us need to have significance and to know that we have the ability to impact our world. The

Creator gave human beings a very important responsibility when He gave us the task of ruling over and maintaining His Creation (Genesis 1:28; Psalm 8:6-8)! People have done incredible things and made unbelievable advances as they have developed technology and processes to manipulate the environment. Unfortunately, we can use these powers for evil as well as for good.

After the Fall our need to have an impact in the world is still a driving force in us, and God continues to offer us the means to meet it. As Christians, God has given us the additional opportunity to advance and build His Kingdom (Romans 10:13-15; Ephesians 4:11-16) and help to restore what has been damaged and ruined by the Fall (Isaiah 61:1-3). God's provision for us to impact our world reinforces the fact that this is an important requirement for our well-being.

CREATED WITH A NEED FOR RELATIONSHIP

One of our most important needs is our requirement for human companionship. In the Garden of Eden, Adam had all his physical needs met and enjoyed close fellowship with God. In spite of this, it was God himself who said, "It is not good for the man to be alone. I will make a helper suitable for him." (Genesis 2:18) God made people in such a way that they need other people.

God helped Adam see his longing for a companion by having him name the animals, and as Adam did this, he realized that there was no one like him (Genesis 2:19,20). Then God created Eve, who had a body of bones and flesh like Adam's, but with some important modifications (Genesis 2:18, 21-22). Adam was obviously pleased (Genesis 2:23).

Many generations later we, the descendants of Adam and Eve, still need companions, and the Bible tells us that God has provided two institutions to help meet this need: the family and the church. Numerous Bible verses discuss the importance of having good, loving human relationships. We are even told that next to loving God, the greatest commandment is to love our neighbor as ourselves (Matthew 22:37-40).

CONCLUSION

God created us with needs. He has also provided us with the means to meet them. Our most important needs are to have close relationships with both God and others, to be able to impact our world for good and to have value and significance in this life. We should not deny these needs but should seek to satisfy them in ways that God intended.

Created With Needs

6

GOAL:

For a disciple to acknowledge that she has needs and to identify some of the specific needs that motivate her behavior.

GETTING STARTED:

The city you live in experiences an ice storm, and you and your family are without power. What needs do you have in this situation?

Food, water—if the pipes freeze, heat, light, communication, etc.

What behaviors do these needs motivate?

Checking on other family members and friends, finding flashlights, candles, batteries, matches, a battery-powered radio, etc.

Transition: In today's lesson, we will learn that we were created with needs, and we will look at how some of these needs motivate our behavior.

STUDYING TOGETHER:

Read Genesis 2:18-22.

1. Did God originally create human beings with needs?

    Yes. Here we see that humans were created with a need for companionship.

    Was this need created before or after the Fall?

    We were created with needs before the Fall.

2. Identify some other primary needs that humans were created with in the following verses. Some of these may be implied needs, not directly stated in the passage.

   Galatians 4:8-9

   We were created with a need for a personal relationship with God. See also Genesis 2:19, 3:8-9 to see that we were created with a capacity to have a relationship with God.

   Genesis 1:26-28; Psalm 8:4-5

   Human beings were created in God's image and, therefore, will always have worth and value. This implies that we have a need for worth and value and that God provided for that need in how He created us.

   Genesis 1:28; Psalm 8:6-8

   Human beings need a purpose and need to have significance. Knowing this, God gave them dominion over the world and the ability to impact their world. Also God gave the command to be fruitful and increase in number.

3. Based on what you've just learned about the primary needs that humans were created with, do you think that needs are necessarily bad?

   No.

   How might having needs actually benefit us?

   Needs are designed to show humans their need for God and to move them toward God as the One who can meet those needs.

4. What problems might humans encounter in trying to meet their own needs?

   Humans may try to deny that we have any needs. We may also try to meet them through means that are not a part of God's design. (See Jeremiah 2:13).

LOOKING AT REAL LIFE:

5. Name two or three needs in each of the following categories. (Needs often overlap into several categories.)

    Physical Needs:

    food, sleep, shelter

    Relational Needs:

    feedback from others, intimacy, communication

    Emotional Needs:

    love, security, affirmation, worth and value

    Spiritual Needs:

    relationship with God, forgiveness, grace, confession of sins

6. Discuss how one or two of these needs might motivate behavior. For example, if a person has no food (a physical need), he will be motivated to spend his waking hours looking for food and ignore other aspects of life.

LOOKING AT MY LIFE:

Write down one area of need in your life and what behaviors that need might motivate.

In closing, ask each group member to pray silently praising God for His ability to meet needs and asking Him to meet the need that they wrote down.

If there is time, ask group members to share their area of need with the group.

Close your prayer time by having the group read Matthew 6:33 aloud together:

> *"But seek first His Kingdom and His righteousness, and all these things will be given to you as well."*

7 Getting Needs Met

What would you think of a medical doctor who tried to treat your illness without really knowing what was wrong with you? When you enter his office he doesn't ask what your symptoms are, doesn't order any tests, but instead, brings in his nurse and begins to put a cast on your leg even though there is nothing wrong with your leg. Undoubtedly you would think, "What a quack this guy is!" and quickly leave to find another doctor. Obviously what you really need is someone who takes the time to understand what your medical needs are and knows how to meet them. We need to take the same approach with all our needs whether they are physical, social, psychological, or spiritual.

God, unlike a doctor, understands all of our needs because He created us with them. He also has provided us with the means to get our needs met. Yet there seems to be confusion in the church today about how our needs are to be met. Some seem to imply (or state directly) that all we need to do is wait and trust God, then He will, in some supernatural way, supply everything we need. It is true that God is the ultimate source who will meet all our needs. We should seek Him, laying our needs before Him. The Bible says He knows our needs and wants to meet them (Matthew 6:25-33). But, will He meet our needs directly or indirectly through other means? The answer to that question depends on what the need is.

> Every one of us can probably point to specific felt needs in our lives that brought us to the point of pursuing God.

God created the world and its inhabitants, and it is through this world that He meets our needs. For instance, we all need air to breathe, and God created air, and He created our lungs to be able to receive and absorb it. He even created us so that we breathe involuntarily. So, God is involved by providing the air, our lungs and the mechanism of breathing, but we are the ones who breathe. I would posit that God is rarely the only one involved in meeting our needs.

One might say it was God alone who provided us with salvation. If that is true, then why isn't everyone a Christian? The answer is that we need to receive the salvation that is offered in order for it to be ours. So, to get this need met we must do something: accept it by faith. A major need is for relationship both with God and with people. God has designed us so that some of our needs can only be met by other people, just as some of our needs can only be met by Him.

Some people believe that it is selfish to focus on our needs. This suggestion may lead a person to conclude that it is never right to think about our own needs. However, thinking about our own needs or even seeking to get them met is not selfish. Selfishness is focusing exclusively on our own needs and ignoring everyone else's. It is being concerned only about oneself. The truth is that we should think about our needs. After all, they are "our" needs; they are not someone else's. And because they are our needs, they are our responsibility, and it is our stewardship to get them met. We should consider our needs and develop a plan to meet them. There are several ingredients involved in getting our needs met.

RECOGNIZE AND ACKNOWLEDGE YOUR NEEDS.

A need must be recognized before it can be addressed. In the last Pocket Principle™ we defined four of our primary needs: our need for God, worth, impact and relationship. But this is not a complete list of our needs. In fact, if one were to sit and brainstorm about the myriad needs that we have, there would be an amazingly long list which would include needs such as: safety, food, shelter, beauty, sexual intimacy, adventure and so on.

Because of concerns about appearing weak, some people have difficulty admitting that they have needs. Yet there is no weakness in admitting that we are just like other human beings! It is important to be honest with ourselves and others and admit our frail, human condition. Such an admission helps us to seek God as we should and to accept help from others when we need it. Many people have suffered needlessly in their lives because they will not admit their need for help.

> We need to be careful to seek to get our needs met in ways that please God.

PUT YOURSELF IN A POSITION TO GET NEEDS MET.

Getting needs met is not an automatic process. It often takes planning and hard work. It is like any other goal we set out to accomplish. It requires something of us. If I want to grow a garden, I cannot just snap my fingers and produce plants. I will need to find a good location, till the ground, plant the seeds, water, fertilize and weed the garden. It is time-consuming, hard work, but it brings a bountiful harvest. Getting our needs met works the same way. It is challenging work, but the benefits are tremendous.

When we are trying to get our relationship needs met, it is not enough to wait for someone else to initiate a friendship with us. We need to take the initiative. We need to go where people are; find people with common interests and needs; reach out and spend time with them; open up and be honest with them about who we are and what is going on in our lives; and be a friend to them.

It may take time to find others that we can feel close to, but in the end, the joy these efforts can bring into our lives is enormous. We need to be careful to seek to get our needs met in ways that please God. In order to meet our needs, we should not demand or pressure people or become involved in immorality or try to please and manipulate others.

Following is a list of healthy ways to get needs met:

1. God will meet many of our needs as we go to Him through spiritual disciplines. Spiritual disciplines are activities such as Bible study, prayer, fellowship and acts of service. As we build these disciplines into our lives, God ministers both to us and through us. He will guide us and give us the insight and wisdom about our needs, among other things.

2. Be willing to ask for and receive help during times of great need and crisis. There are times in our lives when the burdens of life are too heavy for one person to carry. It is at those times that we need to let others know our needs and be willing to let them help us. We also need to help others when they have needs.

3. When we seek help from others, we need to be careful to approach the right kind of people. We need to seek help from people who are willing to help without expecting anything in return and who have our best interest in mind. We also need to seek help from people who are able to help. For instance, we should seek help from a mature Christian when we are in a difficult situation or a counselor when we can't solve a marriage problem.

4. Take action to do something that will lead to needs being met. For instance, we can join a support group to be with people who have gone through a crisis similar to ours. We can make a doctor's appointment when we are physically ill.

RECOGNIZE THAT ALL YOUR NEEDS WILL NOT BE MET PERFECTLY IN THIS LIFE.

Because we live in a fallen, broken world and because sin and temptation will always be with us, our needs will never be perfectly met. They can be substantially met, but never fully met. It is like the old saying, "If you ever find the perfect church, don't join it because you will ruin it." Perfect doesn't exist in this world except in God Himself. So we must develop realistic expectations in this life.

For example, take our need for impact. This need can be met through a ministry or job situation where we are able to use our abilities to make a positive difference or contribution. But we will never do things perfectly or have a perfect result. We need to be satisfied with good enough and not expect perfection.

Ultimately, the perfect meeting of our needs will occur when we are with Christ (Philippians 3:20,21; I Corinthians 15:51-54). When we die physically, we continue to live spiritually and go to be with Christ. What a day that will be! Eventually Jesus will return for His people and all those with Christ will be reunited with their bodies and those who are still alive will be changed in a twinkling of an eye from mortality to immortality. Our new bodies will be perfect and will never wear out.

In the meantime, before Christ returns, we need to recognize needs in our lives that are not being met and develop a realistic plan designed to meet these needs in a healthy way. It is our responsibility and not anyone else's to do this. We need to take responsibility for our own lives and needs, while not ignoring the needs of others.

Getting Needs Met

IMPORTANT to Leader: *Answers and notes to leaders are in gray, italicized text.*

GOAL:

For a disciple to understand how needs are met in a healthy way.

GETTING STARTED:

True/False Quiz

Leader: Tell the students that this quiz is just for their own information. They will score their own quiz, and won't report the results.

1. T/F   God created all of us and created us with needs. Therefore, all we really need is God to meet our needs.

2. T/F   Selfishness is looking only at your own needs to the exclusion of the needs of others.

3. T/F   Our needs will only be met as we minister to others.

Answers

1. *False   The first sentence is true: God did create us all with needs. But the second sentence is false. God will not meet all of our needs Himself directly. His plan is to have others meet our needs also. (Contrast Matthew 6:33 with II Thessalonians 3:10.)*

2. *True   Some people wrongly imply that it is selfish to focus in any way on our own needs (Philippians 2:3-4).*

3. *False   Some of our needs will be met by ministering to others, but not all of our needs.*

Transition: So, how do we get our needs met? To answer this question, we need to understand and apply three ideas.

STUDYING TOGETHER & LOOKING AT REAL LIFE:

First, we need to recognize and acknowledge our own needs.

1. What are some of the needs we discussed in our last lesson?

   Need for companionship, need for a personal relationship with God, need to have value and worth, need to have purpose and significance, etc.

   What are some others?

2. Why is it important to admit that we have needs?

   In order to be intentional about meeting needs we must acknowledge that they exist. As we understand our own needs, we better understand ourselves as well as others, and we can be more effective getting our own needs met and helping meet the needs of others.

Second, we need to put ourselves in a position to get our needs met.

Read Galatians 6:2,4b-5.

3. These verses appear to contradict each other ("carry each other's burden" and "each one should carry his own load"). How might this contradiction be explained?

   The Greek word for "burden" in verse 2 means that the difficulty is too heavy for one person to bear. While the Greek word for "load" in vs. 5 refers to a knapsack-type container which is designed to be carried by one person.

4. What are the 2 principles taught in these verses?

   1:   When a difficulty is too great for one person to handle, he legitimately needs the help of others.

   2:   But when a difficulty is manageable for one person, that person must take responsibility for himself.

5. What are some needs that might fall in each of the categories: "burden" and "load"?

   Too difficult to bear alone:

   Can be managed by one person:

6. What are some healthy ways to get our own needs met?

   Practice the spiritual disciplines (Bible study, prayer, fellowship, service); be willing to receive help in a crisis (e.g. accept offers of help during an illness: food, transportation, etc.); ask for help from appropriate people; choose to do something that may lead to the need being met.

Third, recognize that all of our needs will not be met perfectly in this life.

Read II Corinthians 4:16-18.

7. What do you think Paul means by "outwardly wasting away"?

   Growing old physically, losing mental abilities, have less energy, harder to keep in shape, etc.

8. What does "outwardly wasting away" imply about us getting our needs met?

   It implies that we will never get all our needs met here on earth. Part of the reason we are "outwardly wasting away" is because we are not getting all of our needs perfectly met.

9. What does Paul say we should do in light of this?

   1) Don't lose heart; 2) Allow God to renew us each day; 3) Put our hope in the eternal.

10. Why do you think God designed us in such a way that our needs will not be perfectly met in this life?

    So that we will depend on Him and put our hope in Him and in eternity.

11. How do we live with this fact (our needs not being completely met) and minimize our frustration?

    Develop realistic expectations, don't put hope in this life, use a situation in which needs aren't being met as an opportunity to trust God.

LOOKING AT MY LIFE:

Think of one need (any type) you have in your life right now.

What is a realistic expectation you can have about getting this need met?

What position can you put yourself in to get this need met?

Share your thoughts with the group.

8 Created With Emotions

Recently a woman came to my office for pastoral counseling. Within moments she was sobbing and could not even talk. Eventually she was able to tell me that she had just learned that her husband had had an affair. He wanted to work things out and try to save the marriage, but she was consumed with pain and anger. As she told her story, she vacillated between talking about wanting to kill her husband and wanting to kill herself. By the end of her story, she was considerably calmer and ready to begin the hard work of determining whether her marriage could be saved.

This story brings up some questions. Was it acceptable for this woman to have these strong negative emotions? It is understandable that she would be terribly upset by what had happened. But wouldn't a person who was trusting God have more control over her emotions? How could she talk about killing her husband or herself?

> Without emotion we would live our lives without passion and conviction, like robots.

Sometimes the church sends out confusing messages about how Christians should handle their emotions. Some seem to say that negative emotions, like fear, anger and pain, are always sinful. Anger in particular is often considered sinful. Some say that righteous anger (anger concerning an injustice) is acceptable, but all other anger is wrong. For example, being angry about abortion is all right, but being angry that you made a mistake is not. On the other hand, most Christians think that positive emotions are good. In fact, some people believe that jubilant emotions are an indicator of God's presence. But is God's presence only marked by positive emotions? Can He be present when we have negative emotions as well?

These are important questions to answer. All of us experience a wide range of emotions, and learning their role and function in our lives is essential. We need to understand them and learn to deal with them correctly. Let's look at three principles concerning emotions.

NEGATIVE EMOTIONS ARE NOT EVIL OR SINFUL.

When God created human beings He created them in His image, and this image included emotions, both positive and negative. Scripture tells us that all God created is good (Genesis 1:31), and therefore, all emotions must be good. Another reason we cannot say that emotions we consider negative (e.g. anger, jealousy, fear) are not good is because both God Himself (note God's anger in Psalms 78:31,38,49,50) and Jesus, as a man, experienced these negative emotions. And we know that God did not and cannot sin. Therefore, we must conclude that it is possible to experience negative emotions and not sin. The book of Hebrews describes Jesus experiencing powerful negative emotions:

During the days of Jesus' life on earth, He offered up prayers and petitions with loud cries and tears to the one who could save Him from death, and He was heard because of His reverent submission. (Hebrews 5:7)

Jesus clearly felt the freedom to express his negative emotions to the Father without any fear of reprisal. In fact, the Father accepted these prayers and at one point, sent an angel to minister to Him (Luke 22:41-44).

It is important to understand that emotions, even negative ones, serve many positive roles in our lives. Emotions help us understand what is going on inside of us, and therefore, help us to identify our needs, likes, dislikes, and desires. They also help us experience intimacy. Intimacy occurs when two people connect on an emotional level. If we cannot identify and express our emotions, we cannot connect with someone else on a personal, intimate level. We cannot share our life with a person without letting her know who we are or what is going on inside us.

Emotions also energize and motivate us to do whatever needs to be done. Without emotion we would live our lives without passion and conviction, like robots. For example, love compels me to sacrifice to meet the needs of those I love, while anger motivates me to fix something that is broken or energizes me to remove a blockage that is in the way.

Negative emotions serve the function of alerting us when something is wrong, telling us that something needs attention. Negative emotions are like the warning lights on the dashboard of a car. If the oil light goes on, we had better do something quickly to remedy the situation. Like the physical pain that warns us to take our hand off a hot burner, emotional pain is the warning system that sends us the message that there is a problem that we need to attend to.

We need to attend to our emotions and respond by taking appropriate action. The action may be corrective for negative emotions or repetitive for positive emotions. Our emotions may send us confusing messages, especially when we feel both positive and negative emotions at the same time. In this case, we need to sort out the positive from the negative.

ACTING ON OUR EMOTIONS MAY LEAD TO SINFUL ATTITUDES AND BEHAVIORS.

A young man, who had a wife and small child, had a good job, but he felt that he had been passed over for several promotions. He became increasingly angry and, without consulting anyone or having another job lined up, he quit his job in a fit of anger. Finding a new job was difficult, and while he was looking, he and his wife suffered financial hardship and began fighting about his irresponsibility.

This example demonstrates that acting indiscriminately on emotions, positive or negative, may cause us to hurt others and ourselves. Though emotions are not bad or sinful in and of themselves, how we act based on our feelings may be sinful. For example, a person might feel like punching someone because he is angry. If he acts on his feelings, he may be arrested for assault. Another common mistake is to take out our frustration on a loved one who had nothing to do with the reason for the anger.

Negative emotions serve the function of alerting us when something is wrong, telling us that something needs attention.

It is possible to have positive emotions when doing something wrong or have negative feelings when doing something right. A person who steals something may get a positive rush of adrenaline as a result. Or a mother who sets a limit by telling a child "no" may feel guilty even though she is acting wisely for the welfare of the child. Emotions cannot be trusted to always give a correct reflection of what is right (or wrong) in a situation.

It is wise to process our feelings before acting, to think before we act. There are many ways of processing our emotions. The simplest is to process emotions by choosing to continue feeling them until they go away. This may take quite some time—days or months with a big loss such as the death of someone close. Or it may only last for a short time when the loss is smaller.

In addition, for some people it may also be necessary for them to talk about their feelings with someone they are close to or with God. Talking with someone about our feelings tends to reduce the intensity of the feelings and allows us to make decisions and act in a calmer manner. If someone hurt you, it is important to talk about feelings and not make judgmental remarks about the person.

Another helpful suggestion is to write about what happened and how it made you feel. Writing often enables us to sort out facts and feelings and to make a wise decision about how to respond. All of these processing methods help us slow down, calm down and decide on an appropriate response.

Even though there are no emotions that are wrong, emotions can be expressed in unhealthy or sinful ways; and therefore, it is important for us to know how to process and handle them. When emotions are expressed in healthy ways, the actions we take will be constructive and helpful to others.

DENYING OUR EMOTIONS OR SUPPRESSING THEM CAN LEAD TO SERIOUS PROBLEMS.

Denying or suppressing emotions are unhealthy ways of handling emotions. We often think that if we can avoid them, they will go away. They don't. Instead, they get stored in our bodies in the form of stress. Then the emotions may be triggered (brought to the surface) by a situation similar to the original source of pain, hurt, etc. Thus, a person will overreact to a minor situation because of a past situation. After the overreaction (explosion, tirade, etc.) the person feels better, but has usually damaged his relationships significantly.

People deny their emotions by minimizing them or ignoring them. Many people seek to control their emotions by exerting their will power, but this only works temporarily. Others try to control their emotions by turning to addictions. Addictions involve exchanging an external focus (such as food, sex, work, shopping, exercise, gambling, etc. as well as drugs and alcohol) for an internal focus on the real problem (what is going on inside). Addictions also provide other functions besides distraction. They may make us feel better temporarily or they may numb our emotions.

No matter how hard we try to avoid our feelings, they do not go away. They end up buried inside of us. Scripture warns us not to do this. It tells us to "not let the sun go down while you are still angry." (Ephesians 4:26) In other words, "don't suppress your anger. Rather, deal with it quickly." The same truth applies to all negative feelings.

Ephesians 4:27 says that when we do not deal with our anger in an appropriate and timely way, we give the devil a foothold in our lives. That is, we open ourselves up for attack and for provocation to act out our anger in the wrong way. Any time we allow emotions to build up inside of us we are in danger of becoming overwhelmed by the emotions and of having our judgment clouded. Therefore, we need to learn how to deal with our emotions in appropriate and timely ways.

SUMMARY

In another Pocket Principle™ we will discuss more about how failing to deal appropriately with negative emotions affects us. At this point, it is sufficient to understand that negative emotions are not bad or sinful. When we impulsively act on our negative emotions, without first processing them and thinking about what a godly response would be, then we are in danger of acting sinfully. If we deny or suppress our emotions we are only storing up trouble for later and opening ourselves to temptation.

Created With Emotions

IMPORTANT to Leader: Answers and notes to leaders are in gray, italicized text.

GOAL:

For a disciple to understand the positive function of emotions and to begin thinking about how to deal with those emotions.

GETTING STARTED:

During this past week, what stirred up your emotions the most?

☐ A sporting event you were watching

☐ An argument you were having

☐ A movie you were watching

☐ A book you were reading

☐ Another person's driving

☐ An accomplishment by a family member or friend

☐ Something you purchased

☐ A place you visited

☐ A disappointment you experienced

☐ other: _____

Transition: Throughout each day, we all experience high's and low's in our emotions. In this lesson, we are going to look at the positive aspects of our emotions.

STUDYING TOGETHER:

Read Psalm 13.

1. In verses 1-2, David expresses his heart to God by asking some frank questions. Describe some of the emotions that you see behind David's words.

    Anger, frustration, sadness, sorrow, fear, despair, etc.

2. How do you think most people in our society would view a leader who expressed these types of emotions?

   They may look upon the leader as weak and not worthy of being followed. Or they might appreciate his honesty and vulnerability and feel that he was validating their feelings.

3. Do you think God was surprised when David showed such negative emotions to Him?

   No.

   Why or why not?

   God made human beings in His image which included creating them with emotions. God wired us to be emotional beings. Since all that God created is good, emotions are good.

4. You may be thinking, "But aren't negative emotions such as pain, fear, grief, and anger evil or sinful?" Let's see what the following scriptures indicate about emotions:

   Hebrews 5:7-9

   Jesus, as a man, experienced negative emotions and yet was without sin.

   Psalm 78:31,38,49,50

   God Himself experienced negative emotions and yet was without sin.

5. What important functions can positive and negative emotions serve?

Three primary functions of emotions:

   1. *They help us know ourselves. They help us identify our needs, likes, dislikes, and desires.*

   2. *They help us know others and God. They enable us to experience intimacy by helping us reveal our true selves.*

   3. *Negative emotions tell us when something is wrong and provide motivation and energy to respond. (e.g. Fear tells us to be cautious in a dangerous situation.)*

6. Which of the three functions of emotions that we listed did David experience in Psalm 13?

    Primarily, David was experiencing intimacy with God because he was being honest and revealing his true self.

7. In verses 3-6, how did David deal with his negative emotions toward God?

    David relied on God by asking Him for help. He reminded himself of God's love toward him regardless of the circumstances. He remembered God's faithfulness and goodness toward him in the past. He rejoiced in his future salvation, knowing that his difficult circumstances would not last.

Read Ephesians 4:26.

8. Though we've seen that negative emotions aren't evil in themselves, what warning does Paul give in this verse?

    Be careful because negative emotions can lead to sin. Don't allow them to lead you to sin.

9. In Ephesians 4:26a Paul addresses the issue of acting on our emotions. In 4:26b, what do you think Paul means by "don't let the sun go down on your anger"?

    Denying or suppressing emotions may lead to serious problems. (Addressed in next lesson.)

LOOKING AT REAL LIFE:

10. What are some of the negative attitudes and actions that can result from negative emotions?

    Yelling, cursing, physical violence, lying, sarcasm, etc.

11. What positive functions can negative emotions serve in a person's life?

    Examples: a feeling of isolation when being alone can cause a person to reach out and seek new friendships; frustration with family members can lead to attempts to improve communication; fear of failure at work may encourage diligence and productivity.

LOOKING AT MY LIFE:

Think about the answer to this question: What is the emotion in your life that is the most troubling to you? Silently, lift up this emotion to God, asking Him to help you deal with it in a positive way.

NOTE TO LEADER: Tell group members: It is important to be aware that even if a negative emotion has a positive function you may feel badly (sad, etc.) anyway. Ask group members to do the following if they feel comfortable doing it.

Write down the troubling emotion that you are experiencing on a piece of paper. After the small group session, give it to another group member with your name on it so that over the next week, they can pray that God would help you deal positively with that emotion.

Read aloud the final two verses of Psalm 13 together as a group as your prayer to God.

> *"But I trust in Your unfailing love; my heart rejoices in Your salvation. I will sing to the Lord, for He has been good to me."*

Understanding Emotional Problems

Meet Sarah—

Sarah went through emotional trauma every time her husband left home to go to work. She felt like he was leaving her permanently, even though he had always come home. They had been married for 10 years yet she wrestled with these feelings each time he left home without her.

As I talked with her about her childhood, she told me that she was a quiet, shy child who mainly had been raised in rural areas. However, when she was about to enter junior high school, her father took a job in a big city. Because she was from the country, kids at school made fun of her, and she had a hard time fitting in. This was very traumatic, and she would go home crying every day. Her parents didn't know what to do. They tried talking to her and coaching her. Eventually they told her that she must be doing something wrong or the other kids would like her. They took her to a counselor, and again, she got the message that there was something wrong with her. Nothing changed. In fact, the situation at school got worse.

Her parents finally decided to send her to boarding school in order to give her a new start. Off she went to try to fit in someplace else. But it didn't work. Once again she felt like she didn't fit in. Although she made a few friends, she still felt like the "odd person out." But this time she had no family to rely on. Because her family did not have a lot of resources, Sarah could not see or talk with them very often. Even on holidays she often could not afford to go home and had to stay with a friend. Essentially, Sarah was on her own to take care of herself, cut off from her family. She felt like they had abandoned her.

Now, many years after college and marriage, she still felt abandoned every time her husband left for work. These feelings also affected her relationship with God. She felt that He was distant and unavailable, much like her parents. These experiences led to a whole set of emotional problems that Sarah needed to find some way to deal with.

Sarah is not unique. Everyone experiences emotional pain and problems to some degree. Becoming a Christian does not automatically cause those problems to go away. In fact, they typically get worse if they are not addressed.

There are many ways a Christian's spiritual growth can be affected by unresolved emotional problems. Some Christians are unable to grow spiritually at all. Others are only able to grow to a certain point and then growth stops. There are some who grow to a point and then begin to regress. Still others grow, but their growth is slowed by their emotional problems. Emotionally-based problems do not go away and, in fact, tend to gradually get worse until the person begins to deal with them. Commonly people in their teens and twenties have strong enough coping mechanisms to survive, but their lives and families begin to fall apart in their thirties and forties because of unresolved emotional issues.

Emotional problems tend to be confusing to both the person who is suffering from them and to those in the church that are trying to help. Historically, the church has often not known how to deal with these emotional problems and has focused on the present symptoms instead of the root causes of the problems. The root cause of many emotional problems is found in childhood when a child experiences pain and does not know how to deal with it. The pain remains unresolved and sets off a chain reaction of problems.

UNRESOLVED PAIN IN CHILDHOOD LEADS TO SOME PREDICTABLE PROBLEMS IN A CHILD'S LIFE.

When emotional pain builds up in a child's life and she has no way to deal with it, the pain becomes increasingly overwhelming. The child will *adapt to survive*. She has no choice. She must do something with the pain. Proverbs 15:13 says, "heartache crushes the spirit." This is why the Scriptures admonish parents not to exasperate or embitter their children (Ephesians 6:4; Colossians 3:21). Children are tender and vulnerable, and we need to take great care in how we relate to them. Parents need to provide a safe environment where their children can talk about their feelings.

If a child is not able to process his emotions, there will be several negative results in his life. One result is that he may develop adaptations in order to survive. An adaptation a child often uses is *addictions*. An addiction is anything external that we focus on to avoid what is going on inside. An addiction distracts us from our pain by giving us another focus. Distracting addictions are things such as work, sports, reading, television or video games. Some addictions are mood-altering. We use them to try to feel better: sex, food, drugs, spending or anything that gives us an adrenaline rush. Lastly, there are addictions that numb us like alcohol or sleep. Many people are poly-addicted and use whichever addiction is convenient at the time.

> An addiction is anything external that we focus on to avoid what is going on inside.

Another survival adaptation a child may use is to develop *unhealthy defense mechanisms*. When a child gets hurt on a regular basis, she often develops defense mechanisms to try to avoid getting hurt again. Typical defense mechanisms are denial, people-pleasing, isolating, conflict avoidance, etc.

What happens to the hurtful emotions that a child has but is not able to process? Do they go away? The answer is no. The child *suppresses these negative emotions,* another result of unresolved pain. When emotions are suppressed, they get stored in the child's body in the form of stress. As internal stress builds up through childhood and continues to increase as an adult, it may cause problems such as physical illnesses, emotional explosions, depression, etc.

When hurtful things happen to a child and there is no one to help him make sense out of it, he will usually develop *wrong thinking*, again a result of unresolved pain. He may think that all people are unsafe, that the world is more dangerous than it is or that there is something wrong with him. He may develop those thoughts even further telling himself, "No one loves me"; "No one will protect me"; "I never do anything right"; "I cannot stop this."

One common belief that children tend to develop, when enough bad things happen to them, is that there is something wrong with them. When they make a mistake, they feel like they *are* a mistake. They think they are broken and cannot be fixed. Once a child develops this way of thinking, it is very hard to rectify. The development of this, a *shame-based identity*, also is a result of unresolved pain.

Sarah suffered to some degree from of all these problems. She, like any child, had to adapt to survive the pain that was building up in her life. Once she got to boarding school, she didn't feel as if she had anyone to talk to about her life. Her earlier attempts to talk to her parents and a counselor ended with them accusing her of being the problem. So she just buried the pain on the inside and tried to manage it. She tried to stay busy. If she ever stopped, the powerful feelings she felt were uncomfortable and frightening. Her thinking about people and herself became quite distorted. She felt that there must be something wrong with her and that no one would want to be around someone like her. This led to fewer efforts to make friends and more isolation. Sarah's life seemed to slowly become worse and worse.

UNRESOLVED PAIN IN CHILDHOOD LEADS TO ADDITIONAL PROBLEMS IN AN ADULT'S LIFE.

When children have been injured in their childhood, they carry the unhealthy behaviors, internal stress and wrong thinking into their adult life, which causes more pain. Their injuries keep them immature and lead to unhealthy behavior and thinking. We see this in Sarah's life. The problems in her childhood led to further and deeper problems as an adult. Her life will continue to spin out of control until she begins to address these problems.

There are several typical types of problems that adults will develop when there are unresolved emotional problems from childhood. They will often have *relational problems*. Damage from childhood hinders a person's ability to relate to others in a healthy manner. For example, if there were abusive relationships in a person's past, he may unwittingly seek out similar relationships as an adult, because these kinds of relationships *feel* normal. A person may also become over-controlling because he is afraid of being hurt by others or very passive because he feels powerless to change anything in his life. He may be afraid to get too close to people because he is afraid of being found to be lacking in some way and of being rejected.

It is also common for a Christian with these types of problems to have a *poor relationship with God* as well. All relationships are affected including our relationship with God. For example, emotional issues may lead to a distorted view of God or negative feelings toward Him. Children often project onto God the feelings they have toward their parents. If they felt their parents were distant, they may feel like God is distant. If their parents were extremely critical, they may feel that God is only going to condemn them. They may be unable to *feel* like God loves them. This should not be very surprising since parents have a God-like presence in a child's early life.

> In order to begin to heal and make healthy changes, we need to deal with the root problems.

Another common problem in adulthood is *poor decision-making*. Because of a person's distorted thinking about life and because of addictions, she often makes unwise decisions that are detrimental to her life. Because of a low self-image, she may think she cannot be successful in college or any other kind of school. She may be afraid to try anything challenging, even though she may be more than capable of doing it. She may make poor decisions about finances, relationships, jobs, and many other important areas of life.

Often the pain increases when a person becomes an adult, so the *addictions* also tend to worsen. Adults have more dangerous addictions available to them; and therefore, some addictions may become life threatening.

As stress increases both inwardly and outwardly, people often become clinically *depressed* because the ongoing stress depletes the brain of the chemicals it needs to function correctly. This clinical depression is different from depression caused by a known loss such as the loss of a job, death of a spouse, divorce, etc. In a clinical depression, the person usually doesn't know why he is depressed, and usually, medication and counseling are needed to eliminate the depression.

Although Sarah had become a Christian, she suffered from many of these problems as an adult. She was having relational problems with both God and others, making poor decisions, suffering from addictions and depression. She was addicted to food. She ate to soothe herself, to try to fill the emptiness after her husband left for work. But it didn't work. Instead, she gained weight, which made both her and her husband unhappy.

Sarah also tried to distract herself from the pain by keeping herself constantly busy while her husband was away. But as time passed she became increasingly depressed and isolated. Her workaholism declined, and she spent more and more time in bed. She couldn't concentrate and lost motivation to do anything. Everything became drudgery. As her problems escalated Sarah felt increasingly out-of-control. Her problems were not going to go away without some help. When she was in her thirties, she finally became desperate enough to seek help.

These types of problems tend to get worse and often become overwhelming when the person enters her 30's and 40's. But the tendency is to see the adult behaviors as the problem when they are really only symptoms of the root problems that began in childhood. In order to begin to heal and to make healthy changes, the person needs to deal with the root problems. It is important to understand how emotional problems develop so that we can focus on the root problems (suppressed emotions, false belief systems, unhealthy defense mechanisms, addictions) that began in childhood and not just the symptoms we see in adult life.

Emotionally-based problems are major stumbling blocks in many people's lives, and they must be addressed for a person to reach the kind of spiritual maturity that God has called us to. Traditional approaches to spiritual growth have proven ineffective in bringing about emotional healing. In the next Pocket Principle™ (*Healing From Emotional Problems*) we will discuss what approaches do lead to emotional healing.

Causes And Symptoms Of Emotional Problems

Root Causes of Emotional Problems (in childhood)

Addictions—An addiction is an external focus that enables a person to avoid the pain inside. A child can be addicted to anything: drugs, TV, computer games, sports, food, etc.. Addictions can alter a mood (make a person feel better), dull pain or distract from the pain.

Unhealthy coping (defense) mechanisms—A child develops defense mechanisms to protect himself from getting hurt again. Typical defense mechanisms include: denial, people-pleasing, isolation, conflict avoidance, etc.

Suppressed negative emotions—If a child is unable to process negative emotions and thereby resolve them, the emotions are stored inside in the form of stress. This internal stress may cause problems such as physical illness, emotional explosions, depression, etc. Some signs of suppression are lack of emotion, super-sensitivity, over-reaction, etc.

False belief system—As a child tries to make sense of things happening to her, she usually draws wrong conclusions about herself and the world such as "No one loves me;" "No one will protect me;" "I never do anything right;" "I cannot stop this."

Shame-based identity (a common false belief)—If enough bad things happen to a child, without resolution or explanation, he begins to believe that there is something wrong with him. He believes that he is "broken and cannot be fixed"; he didn't just make a mistake, he is a mistake.

Adult Symptoms of Emotional Problems

Relational problems—Damage from childhood hinders a person's ability to relate to others in a healthy manner. For example, if there were abusive relationships in a person's past, she may unwittingly seek out similar relationships as an adult because these kinds of relationships feel normal.

Poor relationship with God—Just as relationships with others can be affected, a person's relationship with God can also be affected. For example, emotional issues may lead to a distorted view of God or negative feelings toward Him. As a result, a person may stop growing spiritually or even regress.

Poor decisions—Because of a person's distorted thinking about life, he often makes unwise decisions that are detrimental to his life: financially, relationally, professionally, etc.

More serious addictions—Emotions which began in childhood usually intensify in adulthood as the pain worsens. In addition to possible childhood addictions, a person may be addicted to work, spending, shopping, sex, ministry, drugs, alcohol, etc. Some addictions may actually become life-threatening.

Depression—As problems intensify, stress increases, sometimes causing a chemical imbalance in the brain leading to a clinical depression. (This is not the same as a depression caused by a known loss such as the death of a spouse, loss of a job, divorce, etc.)

Understanding Emotional Problems

IMPORTANT to Leader: *Answers and notes to leaders are in gray, italicized text.*

GOAL:

For a disciple to understand that unresolved painful experiences may cause negative consequences such as physical illnesses, addictions, depression, relational problems and distorted thinking.

During the sharing in this group each person needs to understand that the purpose of the group is to **listen, support, and pray,** NOT to give advice and counsel. Also, what is shared in this group is **confidential** and should only be talked about in this group. Knowing that sharing will be kept in confidence encourages openness. We need to be careful that sharing does not deteriorate into gossip.

This study and the next may bring out some emotional issues and unresolved pain in your life or the lives of others. Discipleship small groups like this one are not designed to help people recover from emotional problems or to process their pain. Therefore, if you experience emotional discomfort, it may be wise **to seek outside help.** Please talk with your Leader about this. It may be helpful to read the booklet *How Emotional Problems Develop* (WDA). At the end of that booklet there is a list of options (with definitions) that you may consider: a support group, a restorative group, personal counseling, etc.

At the end of this study, there will be an opportunity for personal sharing. If the sharing is lengthy, we may want to either schedule a separate time to get together and talk, or we may continue the conversation in our next small group meeting.

Important to Leader: Do not be afraid to bring up the issue of an unresolved emotional problem with a person. This might well be one of the most loving, significant influences you can have on a person's life, enabling them to become free to grow in Christlikeness. It is wise to begin developing a list of people and groups that are resources in your community, so that you will be prepared to make a referral when the need arises.

Case Study—Part I

Stephanie grew up in an intact, American, Christian family where the father worked outside the home, and the mother was a homemaker. She has one younger brother. Stephanie's father had a demanding job that required a lot of travel during the week. In addition, he was often at church meetings because he was on the leadership team. But even when he was at home, he usually seemed distracted and unavailable. Neither of the children felt very close to him.

Stephanie's mother was the responsible one at home. She managed the household and the children's activities, but often seemed overwhelmed by it all. Her own negative view of life led her to deal with the children by scolding and criticizing with little praise or positive input. She often felt that she was just barely keeping them under control, and it seemed to Stephanie that it was impossible to please her. Her only interest outside of the home was church, where she was involved in many activities.

Stephanie believed her mother didn't love her and instead, favored her brother. To make herself feel better about herself and her family, she would often sneak food and eat more than she should. The extra weight she gained gave her mother the opportunity to point out Stephanie's "lack of self-control." As an adolescent Stephanie was a good student, tried hard to please others and did not get into trouble. She was hesitant to participate in any extra-curricular activities because she believed that she wouldn't be welcome because in her words, "I never do anything right." Stephanie exerted a lot of emotional effort maintaining a public image that she was always happy and nothing upset her.

Now that Stephanie is an adult, her life is full of struggles. She went to college and earned a degree in education. She met her husband at college, and they married shortly after graduation. Almost immediately she became pregnant, and now has two children in elementary school. Presently, she is in her early thirties and is a homemaker. The family attends church regularly, and Stephanie is involved in a women's Bible study.

Stephanie has always lacked confidence and self-esteem. She dislikes and avoids conflict which has given her husband control over her. If he gets angry at her, she retreats in fear and concludes that she must be a horrible person. She also has problems controlling her children. When they are difficult, she gives in to them. She also experiences guilt and feels that everything that goes wrong is her fault. In the last couple of years she has gained even more weight, and this has made her husband unhappy. She feels depressed and that her life is out of control.

Leader: When everyone has finished reading the case study, lead the group in a discussion. Record their answers on a white marker board, flip chart or overhead projector.

- List the problems you see in *Stephanie's* childhood that you think might have resulted from unresolved pain.

    Possible Answers:
    Believed "I never do anything right."
    Isolated self in high school
    Overate
    Worked to please others
    Worked hard to maintain a favorable public image

    Principle:

    > **Unresolved pain in childhood leads to some predictable problems in the child's life.**

    Typical Problems:

    > ***Addictions*** (e.g. TV, computer games, food, etc.) in order to avoid pain

    > ***Unhealthy defense mechanisms*** (e.g. denial, people pleasing, conflict avoidance)

    > ***Suppressed negative emotions*** (Emotions are stored inside and revealed in the form of stress. Signs: lack of emotion, super-sensitivity, "everything's alright" attitude in the face of real problems, etc.)

    > ***False belief system*** (Making sense of things that have happened by drawing wrong conclusions, e.g. "No one loves me." "I can't do anything right.")

    > ***Shame-based identity*** (Type of false belief system) (Child believes something is fundamentally wrong with him; believes he is a mistake, not just that he made a mistake.)

    (See more details on Exhibit *Causes And Symptoms Of Emotional Problems.*)

- Stephanie's reactions are fairly typical of a child who hasn't been able to resolve (deal with) negative emotions. Which of these problems (the list of Typical Problems above) do you see present in Stephanie's childhood?

- List the problems you see in Stephanie's adult life.

    Possible Answers:
    Avoids conflict
    Low self-esteem
    Fearful
    Feelings of guilt
    Feelings of responsibility for everything that goes wrong
    Overeats
    Depressed
    Overwhelmed
    Doesn't control children
    Husband controls her, and she allows it.

    Principle:

    Unresolved pain in childhood leads to additional problems in adult life.

(See more details on Exhibit *Causes And Symptoms Of Emotional Problems.*)

Typical Problems:

Relational problems (too dependent, fear, avoiding conflict, etc.)

Poor relationship with God (often a distorted view of Him)

Poor decision-making abilities (distorted thinking leads to unwise decisions)

More serious addictions

Depression (stress of problems causes a chemical imbalance in the brain, which leads to a clinical depression)

- Stephanie's adult problems are fairly typical of a person who hasn't been able to resolve (deal with) negative emotions as a child. Which of these problems (the list of Typical Problems above) do you see present in Stephanie's adult life?

- Note any possible connections you see between Stephanie's childhood experiences and her present problems.

Possible Answers:

Brother favored	low self-esteem
Mother critical	low self-esteem
Dad distant	low self-esteem
No good example of dealing with conflict	fear of conflict
No good child-rearing model	too lenient with children
Over-controlling mother	too lenient with children
Negative, critical mother	feels guilty, feels responsible for everything
Mother's, father's and husband's treatment caused pain	depression and addiction: eating problem is escaping or making self feel better

Transition: *Now that we've discussed a situation dealing with how the past affects the present, let's study what the Bible has to say to us about it.*

STUDYING TOGETHER:

Read Exodus 20:4-6, 34:7.

1. What impact can a parent's sin potentially have on future generations?

   A parent's poor choices and sinful actions can negatively affect many generations in significant ways. (Also see Ephesians 6:4; Colossians 3:21.)

2. According to Exodus 20:6, what kind of impact can obedient and loving actions have on future generations?

   Loving choices and obedient actions have a far greater positive effect than sinful, poor choices and actions do.

LOOKING AT REAL LIFE:

3. Briefly describe a situation in which you can see that a person's past is affecting their present behavior/life. (Be careful to respect the privacy of others by not revealing who you are talking about. Also, do not share anything that is shared within this group outside of the group so people will feel free to be honest and open.)

LOOKING AT MY LIFE:

Is there a painful experience in your past that might still be affecting you in the present? If you feel comfortable doing so, please share that experience with the group. Close in prayer.

Healing From Emotional Problems

God is in the business of healing. He came to heal us from the damage of sin, as well as to enable us to grow in our relationship with Him. In fact, if we do not heal from the damage sin has caused in our lives, our spiritual life will almost certainly be impaired.

At the very beginning of Jesus' ministry, He quoted from the Old Testament Book of Isaiah (Luke 4:18-19) defining what His ministry would be like, what it would include. It is very clear that Jesus' ministry would be a ministry of healing as well as of salvation.

*The Spirit of the Sovereign Lord is on Me,
because the Lord has anointed Me
to preach good news to the poor.
He has sent Me to bind up the brokenhearted,
to proclaim freedom for the captives
and release from darkness for the prisoners,
to proclaim the year of the Lord's favor
and the day of vengeance of our God,
to comfort all who mourn,
and provide for those who grieve in Zion—
to bestow on them a crown of beauty instead of ashes,
the oil of gladness instead of mourning,
and a garment of praise instead of a spirit of despair.
They will be called oaks of righteousness,
a planting of the Lord for the display of His splendor.
They will rebuild the ancient ruins
and restore the places long devastated;
they will renew the ruined cities
that have been devastated for generations.
(Isaiah 61:1-4)*

In these verses an interesting scenario is presented. The prophet Isaiah is speaking about One who will preach the good news of the gospel, free those who are in bondage, heal the brokenhearted and comfort those who mourn. All these are healing ministries. The person who will come to do this is Jesus Himself (as He made evident both through His statements and His ministry). The text goes on to say that those who have experienced these healing ministries of the Lord will become "oaks of righteousness" which means that their righteousness will be their strength. He goes on to say that these "oaks of righteousness" will be the very ones that will restore what is ruined in the culture. They will become powerful change agents in their cultures.

He makes it clear that only those who have come to know Christ and have been set free from their emotional issues will impact the world for God. It is only those who have been healed from their spiritual poverty, emotional wounds, bondage to addictions, and distorted thinking who will be able to help others be restored from the damages of sin, renew their minds, restore broken relationships and build healthy families.

How does this healing come about? Believers can deal with emotional issues by completing the following process.

IDENTIFY EMOTIONAL PROBLEMS.

The following list describes unhealthy ways emotions may affect us, thus indicating that something needs correction or healing. See if any of these items are descriptive of your experience. (Can also be found in the Exhibit, *Evaluating And Dealing With Emotional Problems*.)

1. You are numb and do not feel your emotions.
2. The emotions you feel are mainly negative.
3. You tend to overreact or be supersensitive in certain situations.
4. You do not know how to express your emotions appropriately.
5. You are afraid of certain emotions.
6. You try to distract yourself so you will not feel certain emotions.
7. You believe that certain emotions are bad and that you should not have them.
8. You are often confused by some of your emotions.
9. You are depressed for no clear reason.
10. You do not know how to deal with pain.
11. You are bitter, negative or simply unable to enjoy life.
12. You take out your anger on people that are not the source of the anger.
13. You are not able to control your expression of anger.
14. You feel out of control most of the time.
15. You are afraid to stop and be silent with just your emotions.

Everyone has emotional issues to some degree, at some time. This is part of being human and living in a fallen world. If even one of these statements describes you, it indicates that there is an emotional issue you need to deal with. If more than one of these statements describes you, there are more serious emotional issues to attend to. Although these statements indicate that something is wrong, they do not tell what is wrong. Determining that will take more time and careful analysis.

UNDERSTAND THE HEALING PROCESS.

Emotional issues may affect many areas of a person's life. Therefore, we must look at many areas of life in order to understand the healing process. Following is a list of actions that may need to be taken for a person to heal from emotional problems.

Stop abusive relationships—If a person continues in a hurtful relationship, emotional problems will worsen. It will take all of his energy to just survive the relationship, and therefore, there will not be any energy left to work on emotional issues. In hurtful relationships, self-worth is destroyed, distorted thinking patterns emerge, and the person is cut off from what he needs. Therefore, it is necessary to stop these relationships or change them in order for healing to occur (Psalm 1:1).

Control addictions—Severe addictions hinder a person's ability to deal with emotions because these addictions exist, at least in part, to keep the person from feeling their painful emotions. Addictions also destroy relationships and are an escape from the real issues of life. Addictions must be brought under control before a person can make any progress in healing (Romans 8:12,13).

Learn to view and express emotions properly—Emotional problems begin primarily from not being able to deal with emotions appropriately; and therefore, it is crucial that a person learn about emotions and develop the ability to deal with them and express them appropriately (Ephesians 4:26).

Grieve pain and losses—Everyone needs to learn how to grieve losses from both the present and past. A person with emotional problems almost always has unresolved emotions from the past that are stored internally. These emotions must be felt and released, a process called grieving, for the person to heal. (Isaiah 61:2,3; Matthew 5:4).

Understand needs and how to get them met appropriately—God has created everyone with needs, and whether or not a person is aware of her needs, she is still driven to meet them. In order to live a healthy life, we need to be able to identify our needs and learn healthy ways to meet them (Matthew 6:32).

Learn to distinguish between healthy and unhealthy thinking and behavior—People who are hurting tend to think in extremes. They may discount positive things that happen or maximize bad things that happen. They may jump to conclusions with little evidence or deny that painful events bother them. Behaviors follow our beliefs, so if our thinking is wrong, it will lead to unhealthy behaviors as well. In order to become healthy, one must develop correct thinking about oneself, others and God (Romans 12:2).

Develop healthy relationships and a good support system—One of the primary ways God meets the needs of people is through relationships with others. Therefore, we need to be able to develop healthy relationships. Because no one person can meet all the needs of another person, we need to have a network of good relationships, a support system. People were not created to live in isolation, and all of us need caring relationships, validation and helpful feedback in order to function well in life (Hebrews 10:24,25).

Learn to grow spiritually—Emotional healing and spiritual growth occur simultaneously. You cannot have one without the other. Therefore, it is important to focus on both at the same time. They need to be intermixed. Jesus wants to help you grow spiritually and heal emotionally and relationally at the same time (Matthew 5:3,4).

The first two actions in the list (stop abusive relationships and control addictions) must be addressed first because failing to address them will prevent the other six from happening. The last six do not happen in any particular sequence. Rather, they may occur simultaneously during a group session or in personal counseling. In order to explain them and show their importance, they are noted here as separate issues.

One might ask: Why is this so complex? Why are there so many areas that need to be addressed for a person to get better? The answer is that people are complex. We are made up of several interrelated systems: physical, emotional, mental, relational and spiritual. When something goes wrong in one of these systems, the others are also affected because everything about us is interconnected.

It is like a problem I recently had with my car. A rock was temporarily caught between a pulley and a belt and stretched the belt. Because the belt was not tight enough, it began to slip on the alternator. Since the alternator wasn't turning fast enough, the battery ran down. Neither the battery nor the alternator was producing enough electricity to run the car so the lights would not work and the engine would not run. When one part failed to function properly, other parts that were dependent on it also began to fail. It takes a great deal of work to align all the systems in our lives. But when our lives begin to function correctly, it leads us to new levels of maturity and enables us to function in a healthy and effective manner.

SEEK OUTSIDE HELP TO DEAL WITH EMOTIONAL PROBLEMS.

People often need help dealing with emotional problems. In fact, God never intended for us to deal with them alone. Scripture tells us to, "confess your sins to each other and pray for each other so that you may be healed." (James 5:16)

It is usually only when we can be totally honest, in the midst of safe people, that healing will take place. When we bring our struggles out into the open they lose much of their power over us, and we can find needed support and help to overcome them.

There are many sources of help for emotional issues. Sometimes several of these sources need to be employed at once, or over a period of time. The following is a list of such sources: (in no particular order)

1. Personal counseling

2. Support groups—These groups focus on a single issue that all the group members have in common (e.g. death of a child, divorce, etc.)

3. Addiction groups—These are also called 12 step groups. They focus on controlling a specific addiction. For example Alcoholics Anonymous focuses on controlling alcohol. Over Eaters Anonymous focuses on controlling eating. There are groups for almost any kind of addiction.

4. Restorative groups—These groups focus on developing emotional and relational health. Their goal is to help people learn how to handle emotions correctly, grieve past losses, think correctly and develop needed relational skills.

5. Involvement with the body of Christ—The church can provide a lot of help in the healing process. We can find encouragement and help to grow spiritually. A growing knowledge of the Word of God teaches us how to think right. It can also provide safe and supportive people who will encourage us and hold us accountable.

6. Medication—Stress due to emotional problems can cause brain chemical imbalances and other physical problems that may require medication. (For example, a common problem is the development of clinical depression that requires an anti-depressant to restore brain chemical balance.)

There is always hope for healing from emotional problems because nothing is impossible with God (Luke 1:37). God wants to transform our lives from the inside out. If we change on the inside, external aspects of our lives will change also. Some people are able to effectively apply principles of restoration to their own lives after they hear or read them. Others need outside help over a longer period of time before their healing is complete. Regardless, it is the people who work hard at all aspects of restoration and who look to God for strength and guidance in the process who make the fastest progress in the restorative process. Becoming restored emotionally and relationally is hard work, and there are no shortcuts.

Evaluating And Dealing With Emotional Problems

CHECKLIST OF INAPPROPRIATE WAYS TO HANDLE NEGATIVE EMOTIONS

☐ You are numb and do not feel your emotions.

☐ The emotions you feel are mainly negative.

☐ You tend to overreact and be supersensitive in certain situations.

☐ You do not know how to express your emotions appropriately.

☐ You are afraid of certain emotions.

☐ You try to distract yourself so you will not feel certain emotions or you do unhealthy things to alter your moods. People often fixate on things outside themselves (food, sex, work, cleaning, shopping, spending, alcohol, drugs, etc.) in order to avoid dealing with internal, painful emotions.

☐ You believe that certain emotions are bad and that you should not have them.

☐ You are often confused by some of your emotions.

☐ You are depressed for no clear reason.

☐ You do not know how to deal with pain.

☐ You are bitter, negative or simply unable to enjoy life.

☐ You take out your anger on people that are not the source of the anger.

☐ You are not able to control your expression of anger.

☐ You feel out of control most of the time.

Understanding The Healing Process

Emotional problems affect many areas of a person's life. The following is a list of actions that typically need to be taken.

1. Stop abusive relationships. If a person continues in a hurtful relationship, emotional problems worsen. Self-worth is destroyed; a person struggles to merely survive; distorted thinking patterns emerge; a person is cut off from what he needs, etc. (Psalm 1:1).

2. Control addictions. Severe addictions hinder a person's ability to deal with her emotions, prevent her from getting needs met (see Pocket Principle™ *Created With Needs*), and destroy relationships. Her life worsens in all aspects (Romans 8:12,13).

3. Learn to view and express emotions properly. Instead of repressing emotions or improperly venting them, a person needs to understand them and process them appropriately (Ephesians 4:26).

4. Grieve pain and losses, especially from the past. If a person has unresolved losses from her past, she needs to learn how to grieve those losses and let go of them (Isaiah 61:2,3; Matthew 5:4).

5. Understand needs and how to get them met appropriately. Whether or not a person is aware of his needs, he is still driven by them. Therefore, it is imperative to define real needs and understand how to meet them (Matthew 6:32).

6. Learn to distinguish between healthy and unhealthy thinking and behavior. People who are hurting tend to think in extremes (e.g. "Everybody hates me." "It's all your fault. You made me do it.") In order to become healthy a person must develop correct thinking about himself, others and God (Romans 12:2).

7. Develop healthy relationships and a healthy support system. People were not created to live in isolation. We need caring relationships, validation and helpful feedback in order to function well in life (Hebrews 10:24,25).

8. Learn to grow spiritually. Emotional healing and spiritual growth occur simultaneously. Therefore, we must focus on spiritual growth as we heal emotionally.

Seeking Outside Help To Deal With Emotional Problems

There are many sources of help for emotional issues. Sometimes several of the following need to be employed at once or over a period of time.

1. Personal counseling

2. Support groups—These groups focus on a single issue that all the group members have in common (e.g. death of a child, divorce, etc.)

3. Addiction groups—These are also called 12 step groups. They focus on controlling a specific addiction. For example Alcoholics Anonymous focuses on controlling alcohol. Over Eaters Anonymous focuses on controlling eating. There are groups for almost any kind of addiction.

4. Restorative groups—These groups focus on developing emotional and relational health. Their goal is to help people learn how to handle emotions correctly, grieve past losses, think correctly and develop needed relational skills.

5. Involvement with the body of Christ—The church can provide a lot of help in the healing process. We can find encouragement and help to grow spiritually. A growing knowledge of the Word of God teaches us how to think right. It can also provide safe and supportive people who will encourage us and hold us accountable.

6. Medication—Stress due to emotional problems can cause brain chemical imbalances and other physical problems that may require medication. (For example, a common problem is the development of clinical depression that requires an anti-depressant to restore brain chemical balance.)

While some people need one or several of these resources in order to heal emotionally, others may only need to apply principles of recovery in the normal growth process.

Healing From Emotional Problems

10

GOAL:

For a disciple to understand some of the things a person can do in order to begin to resolve emotional problems.

During the sharing in this group each person needs to understand that the purpose of the group is to **listen, support, and pray,** NOT to give advice and counsel. Also, what is shared in this group is **confidential** and should only be talked about in this group. Knowing that sharing will be kept in confidence encourages openness. We need to be careful that sharing does not deteriorate into gossip.

Just as with the last study, this study may bring out some emotional issues and unresolved pain in your life or the lives of others. Discipleship small groups like this one are not designed to help people recover from emotional problems or to process their pain. Therefore, if you experience emotional discomfort, it may be wise **to seek outside help.** Please talk with your Leader about this. It may also be helpful to read the booklet *How Emotional Problems Develop* (WDA). At the end of that booklet there is a list of options (with definitions) that you may consider: a support group, a restorative group, personal counseling, etc.

At the end of this study, there will be an opportunity for personal sharing. If the sharing is lengthy, we may want to either schedule a separate time to get together and talk, or we may continue the conversation in our next small group meeting.

*Important to Leader: **Do not be afraid to bring up the issue of an unresolved emotional problem with a person.** This might well be one of the most loving, significant influences you can have on a person's life, enabling them to become free to grow in Christlikeness. It is wise to begin developing a list of people and groups that are resources in your community, so that you will be prepared to make a referral when the need arises.*

GETTING STARTED:

Allow each group participant to silently read the following case study about resolving emotional problems. The goal here is to show examples of what a person needs to do in order to heal from emotional problems. This case study also demonstrates that if emotional problems are not dealt with they will not get better and usually get worse.

Case Study—Part 2

Stephanie's life seemed to be spinning out of control. She realized that she needed to get help. Not knowing what else to do, she made an appointment with her pastor. He soon realized that Stephanie's problems were more than he could handle so he referred her to a Christian counselor. The counselor was able to help Stephanie see that most of her problems stemmed from things that happened in her childhood that had not been resolved. Her childhood experiences had affected the way she thought about herself and left her with ineffective ways of dealing with life.

The counselor helped Stephanie take several important steps. First, he referred her to a psychiatrist who prescribed anti-depressant medication. He also helped her deal with the deep anger she had toward her mother. The counselor knew that she also had issues with her father because he had not been there for her, but believed that those could wait until later. Her issues with her mother were more prominent at this time. The counselor also introduced Stephanie to an Overeaters Anonymous group to help her gain control over her eating. It was important that she stop using food to medicate her emotions. Instead, she needed to learn how to feel her emotions and grieve her losses so that the negative emotions she had stuffed inside could be released and dissipate (go away).

It took about nine months for Stephanie to work through these initial issues, and then the counselor started helping her develop healthier ways of thinking about herself and of dealing with her mother, husband and children. He also suggested that she join a restorative group to help reinforce the new thinking and behavior in her life.

The process of turning her life around was difficult and painful as well as time-consuming, but Stephanie did it. Eventually she began to feel better about herself. Her family life improved because she was relating to the members of her family in healthier ways. Her husband even went with her to marriage counseling for a while. The greatest surprise to her was how much her relationship with God improved.

After everyone has finished reading the case study, lead your group in the following discussion:

- What helped Stephanie get better?

  Possible answers:
  Sought help; went to pastor and counselor
  Cooperated with the counselor
  Took medication
  Went to OA group
  Developed better thinking patterns (restorative group)
  Processed her emotions, grieved losses
  Persevered; was patient; realized it takes time

- What were the results (stated and implied) of Stephanie's cooperation with the counselor and her perseverance?

  Possible answers:
  Developed better relationships with mother, husband, children
  Healthier emotionally (not depressed)
  Better eating habits
  Better relationship with God
  Healthier view of self
  Now she is ready to begin to deal with her issues with her unavailable father

Leader: Read through the Exhibit Understanding The Healing Process *together and discuss any questions group members may have.*

Also read through the Exhibit Seeking Outside Help.

Transition: *Now that we've discussed an example of how a person can heal from emotional problems, let's study what the Bible has to say to us about it.*

STUDYING TOGETHER:

Read Isaiah 61:1-4.

1. What do verses 1-3 indicate about God's desire to heal emotional hurts?

    God is interested in healing our emotional hurts.

2. According to verse 3, what will be the result of healing in people's lives?

    People will become "oaks of righteousness." In other words healing will result in strength.

3. According to verse 4, what is another effect of healing?

    People who are healed are able to help restore the devastation in the lives of others.

Read Ecclesiastes 7:3; Matthew 5:4.

4. According to these verses, what is a necessary part of emotional healing?

    Grieving.

    Have group members silently read Psalm 4 and 7.

5. What do both of these Psalms begin with?

    Grieving

    How do they both end?

    With praise.

    Why do you think there is a connection between "grieving" and "praising"?

LOOKING AT REAL LIFE:

6. Based on your life and your experience with other people, how common do you think these emotional problems are?

   Very common

7. What do you think the church's role should be in addressing these problems?

   1) Should be a safe place for people with emotional problems 2) Help people identify emotional problems in their life 3) Help people find help either in the church or refer for counseling, a restorative group or other outside agency.

LOOKING AT MY LIFE:

Recall the personal emotional problem you identified last week ("a painful experience in your past that is still affecting the present"). What specific step can you take this week to begin to address that problem? If you feel comfortable doing so, share with the group and pray for each other.

Leader: Remind the group that the growth process is slow and requires patience. Emotional healing and growth take time.

What's Next?

We hope you enjoyed this study.
You may be wondering: "So, what's next?"
I'm glad you asked.

If your group has benefited from their experience with this study, we suggest that you continue the Cornerstone series. The next group of studies in this series is *Growing Spiritually* (10 studies). [The first group of studies in Cornerstone, *Laying Foundations* is *Knowing God* (10 studies). If you have not already done this study, we suggest that you do it next.] All of these studies follow the same format as *Understanding People*. (See link on next page.)

Because you have chosen to lead, we want to do all we can to support you. In addition to the materials provided in this workbook, we would like to also offer you a free download of the Teaching Outlines for *Understanding People*.
(See link on next page.)

If you want to study materials that will help you grow as a leader, you might be interested in the *Small Groups Manual* (WDA) or the *Life Coaching Manual* (WDA), both can be found on the WDA store at www.disciplebuilding.org. (See link on next page.)

Also, **on the WDA website you will find explanations about the meaning of the different Phases I through V.** If you want to understand more about progressive growth there is a free download on our website called *Disciple Building: A Biblical Framework*. This explains the biblical basis for our disciple building process. (See links on next page.)

If you want to understand more about the Restorative Ministry, there is a free download entitled *How Emotional Problems Develop* on our website. The Restorative Ministry addresses relational and emotional needs that affect a disciple's ability to grow spiritually. (See links on next page.)

We look forward to a long association with you as you seek and follow our Lord, and grow in Christ using WDA Materials.

Bob Dukes

Links

Knowing God, *Understanding People* and *Growing Spiritually:*

www.disciplebuilding.org/product-category/laying-foundations-phase-2

Free Teaching Outlines for *Understanding People:*

http://www.disciplebuilding.org/materials/understanding-people-teaching-outlines-free-download/

Small Groups Manual and *Life Coaching Manual:*

www.disciplebuilding.org/materials/description_materials/4

www.disciplebuilding.org/product-category/leadership-manuals

Meaning of Phases I-V:

www.disciplebuilding.org/about/phases-of-christian-growth/2

Free Download of *Disciple Building: A Biblical Framework:*

www.disciplebuilding.org/store/leadership-manuals/disciple-building-a-biblical-framework

Free Download of *How Emotional Problems Develop:*

www.disciplebuilding.org/ministries/restorative-ministry

About the Restorative Ministry:

www.disciplebuilding.org/ministries/restorative-ministry

About WDA

WDA's mission is to serve the church worldwide by developing Christlike character in people and equipping them to disciple others according to the pattern Jesus used to train His disciples.

Organized as Worldwide Discipleship Association (WDA) in 1974, we are based in the United States and have ministries and partners throughout the world. WDA is a 501c(3) non-profit organization funded primarily by the tax-deductible gifts of those who share our commitment to biblical disciple building.

WDA is committed to intentional, progressive discipleship. We offer a flexible, transferable approach that is based on the ministry and methods of Jesus, the Master Disciple Builder. By studying Jesus' ministry, WDA discovered five phases of Christian growth. The Cornerstone series focuses on the first and second phases, Phase I: Establishing Faith and Phase II: Laying Foundations (*Knowing God, Understanding People* and *Growing Spiritually*). This series addresses the needs of a young believer or a more mature believer who wants a review of foundational Christian truths.

The remaining phases are: Phase III: Equipping for Ministry; Phase IV: Developing New Leaders and Phase V: Developing Mature Leaders.

For more information about WDA please visit our website: www.disciplebuilding.org.

If you are interested in seeing other WDA materials, please visit the WDA store: www.disciplebuilding.org/store.

Made in the USA
San Bernardino, CA
03 November 2014